Modern French Poetry

a bilingual anthology

Modern French Poetry

a bilingual anthology

edited and translated by

Patricia Terry and Serge Gavronsky

Columbia University Press

New York and London 1975

Library of Congress Cataloging in Publication Data
Main entry under title:

Modern French poetry.

   English and French on opposite pages.
   Bibliography: p. 235
   1. French poetry—Translations into English.   2. English poetry—
Translations from French.   3. French poetry—19th century.
4. French poetry—20th century.
I. Terry, Patricia   II. Gavronsky, Serge.
PQ1170.E6M57   841'.008   75-17893
ISBN 0-231-03957-3
ISBN 0-231-03958-1 pbk.

Acknowledgments

We wish to express our thanks to members of the Barnard French department, particularly Professors LeRoy C. Breunig, Helen Bailey and Tatiana Greene, who have offered suggestions and encouragement to this book. We are grateful to Professor Renée Geen not only for painstaking readings and recommendations, but also for her services as arbitrator of otherwise unresolvable disputes. The editors of this book are especially indebted to Professor Maurice Z. Shroder who offered numerous highly illuminating comments. His collaboration led to the inclusion of three Mallarmé translations that bear his initials.

P.T. and S.G.

Table of Contents

Table of Contents

Modern French Poetry

a bilingual anthology

Introduction

Poetry is the variety of literature most particularly subject to inappropriate ways of reading. Its purposes, methods, and accomplishments tend to seem obscure, even undefinable. It has been considered an inconsequential pastime, an outlet for personal, often banal, experiences of life and love, an awesome semi-sacred utterance. The poems in this collection correspond to different criteria: they are addressed to the intellect as well as to the emotions; despite their varying degrees of complexity, they may all be apprehended in their own, self-contained, words; and all of them should be evaluated in terms of the dynamic experience they provide, and not as monuments of literary history.

Poetry is language compressed to its highest efficiency. The words of a poem operate simultaneously on different levels—intellectually, aesthetically, semantically, in relation to responses they may be expected to evoke, in relation to each other. And, contrary to popular opinion, language of poetic density can function effectively only if its complexity is consciously recognized. The special techniques that may be involved in the writing of poetry are means for increasing the potency of language. We have included introductory material on French versification, rhetoric and poetics, not to encourage a distracting and illusory faith in the usefulness of terminology, but to facilitate the reading of poems on their own terms.

The requirements that a poem be self-contained and of interest as literature, rather than as doctrine or entertainment, indicate little of the kind of experience it may in fact be expected to provide. The greatest poems do not change anything, neither political commitment, nor human nature, nor the basic conditions of life on earth. Nor do they ask us to be

moved by experience which does not go beyond the merely personal. But a poem intensifies our awareness of reality while moving it wholly into the mind; it makes us react to death, loneliness, the texture of apples or smoke as to something of value. It may also make us aware that the most basic commitment of a poem is to language itself.

Poets have always acknowledged the assistance of non-rational elements, whether promptings of the Muse, the subconscious, or the spontaneous self-ordering of words. Analysis of poetic technique indicates that it is only partially directed to the intellect. The best rhymes involve compatible meanings, but the repetition of sounds in a predictable pattern has its own effect, creating an illusion of inevitability, and adding intensity to the words it unites. A prose poem, though it rejects one set of formal rules, imposes another kind of rigor which can, for example, make the emphatic statement of the conclusion equal in power to the last line of a sonnet.

The interplay of sound, rhythm, meaning, and the physical position of the words on the page does more than contribute to the statement of the poem: it *is* the poem. Each word should involve its own full range of meanings as well as its relationship to all the other words of the poem. Change in any part changes the whole; it is in that sense an organic structure.

Poets indicate that the poem is for them too a voyage of discovery, that the significance the poem gives to experience was not completely known to them at the outset. The words of the poem are not a record of that exploration, they are identical with it. That is why the reader must make a conscious effort to align himself with the text, to focus on the words in the order in which they occur. He must participate actively, but without allowing himself to be distracted by associations of ideas relevant only to his personal and prior experience. A poem may present similes and metaphors as facts, but to be

experienced as such they will have to fuse in the reader's mind as they did in the poet's. A metaphor may bring about a new unity which illuminates both its parts by the identical emotional response the poet, and after him the reader, may have to dissimilar things, or the unifying quality may be visual, tactile, dynamic, or abstract; but there must *be* one. To become conscious of the unifying factor is to increase not weaken the effect of the poem.

The themes of poetry differ in their apparent importance, but they are really occasions for one underlying subject: the interaction of the mind, expressing itself through language, and the reality of which it is a part. The process of writing a poem will make the ostensible subject subordinate, and may even destroy it. Writing of *ennui* the poet becomes purposeful, committed: Baudelaire's analogy of the sky weighing down on us like a heavy lid is experienced as life-enhancing rather than crushing. The poem, regardless of theme, becomes its own subject. It is a celebration of language.

P.T. and S.G.

French Versification

How to Read French Verse

1.1. The accents

The accents in French verse fall on the last syllable pronounced: the final *e* is excluded.

> example: J'ai longtemps habité sous de vastes por*tiques*

> Baudelaire: *La Vie antérieure*

1.2. The accent within a line of verse

When there is a group of words syntactically joined, as in a line of traditional poetry, the individual word loses its accent. Only the final syllable of a group is accented.

> example: Je suis *belle,* ô mor*tels!* comme un rêve de *pierre,*

> Baudelaire: *La Beauté*

1.3. The melody of a French line of verse

French verse has levels of pitch. Some syllables are pronounced on a higher level. Thus, at the end of a phrase in two parts, or after an interrogative or an exclamatory construction, the voice rises.

> example: O la face cend*rée,* l'écusson de *crin,* les bras de cris*tal!*

> Rimbaud: *Being Beauteous*

1.4. The distribution of accents

French poetry avoids a monosyllabic series which would underscore the absence of any cadence. However, for comical effects or contrastual ones, the poet may use such a series deliberately.

>   example: Il n'y a pas de nuit pour nous

>   Eluard: *Printemps*

1.5. The temporal factor

An accentuated syllable lasts longer than another. The longest time pause corresponds to the accented syllable (see 1.2.).

>   example: Ah! même dans la *mort* je souffre d'insom*nies*

>   Supervielle: "Perdu parmi les
>   pas . . ."

1.6. The mute *e*

Though the final *e* is always silent, it does serve to elongate the preceding sound. (see 2.4.).

>   example: L'hiver à une pareille altitude m'effraie

>   Reverdy: *Allégresse*

1.7. The role of silences

As in music, the silences are significant in the reading of a French line of verse. The silences that follow accentuated syllables, as they reoccur throughout the poem, contribute to the distribution of harmonic impressions. They also correspond to fixed structural elements (see 6.1., 6.2., 6.4.).

>   example: La chair est triste, hélas! et j'ai lu tous les livres

>   Mallarmé: *Brise marine*

The Structure of the French Verse

2.1. The syllabic count: dieresis (une diérèse)

By tradition, when two vowels are together and the first one is an *i*, a *y*, a *u*, or an *o* that can be transformed into a *j*, *w*, *y*, they are pronounced as two separate syllables.

> example: li-on; jou-et

2.2. The syllabic count: synaeresis (une synérèse)

When two vowels form a single vowel, because of their Latin roots, they are pronounced as a single unit.

> example: noir, foi

2.3. The syllabic count: the mute *e*

Until the sixteenth century, the mute *e* was voiced. Thereafter, this practice was formally prohibited. The mute *e* within the line of verse is elided if it is followed by either a vowel or a mute *h*.

> example: Quelque fuite atroce de vous.

> > Verlaine: *Spleen*

> example: Dans leur double horizon inerte indifférent

> > Eluard: "Le front aux vitres . . ."

2.4. The mute *e* between two consonants

When the mute *e* is between two consonants, it is always pronounced.

> example: —Mélancoliques pèlerins,—

> > Verlaine: *Le Faune*

2.5. The mute *e* after a vowel in a word

When the mute *e* is part of syllable, it is no longer counted.

> example: De grands lierres s'étiraient
>
> > Follain: *Le Feu*

2.6. The mute *e* at the end of a line of verse

The final *e* is never pronounced nor is it counted at the end of a line.

The Richness of French Rhymes

3.1. Weak rhymes (une rime pauvre)

A weak rhyme occurs when there is a single identical sound.

> example: Et si je ne sais plus tout ce que j'ai véc*u*
> C'est que tes yeux ne m'ont pas toujours v*u*.
>
> > Eluard: "La courbe de tes
> > yeux . . ."

3.2. Sufficient rhymes (une rime suffisante)

A sufficient rhyme contains either a consonant followed by a vowel:

> example: —Ton cœur bat-il toujours à mon seul *nom*?
> Tourjours vois-tu mon âme en rêve?—*Non*.
>
> > Verlaine: *Colloque sentimental*

or a vowel followed by a consonant:

> example: Leurs yeux sont morts et leurs lèvres sont
> m*olles,*
> Et l'on entend à peine leurs par*oles.*
>
> > Verlaine: *Colloque sentimental*

3.3. Rich rhymes (une rime riche)

A rich rhyme has at least three similar sonorous elements.

> example: Je partirai! Steamer balançant ta m*âture,*
> Lève l'ancre pour une exotique *nature!*

> Mallarmé: *Brise marine*

3.4. Traditional rules of rhyme

Historically, French rules of rhyme have prohibited rhyming a singular with a plural since the text was meant equally for the eyes and for the ear.

3.5. Modern practices

Very little attention is given to structuring rhymes in contemporary French poetry, especially after the mid-nineteenth-century excesses of the Parnassian school. French poets now tend to reject both rhyme schemes and syllabic count.

The Disposition of Rhymes

4.1. The couplet (une rime plate)

The rhyme scheme is aa, bb, cc, etc.

> example: Il faut trouver d'autres thèmes,
> Plus mortels et plus suprêmes.
> Oh! bien, avec le monde tel quel,
> Je vais me faire un monde plus mortel!

> Laforgue: *Simple agonie*

4.2 Enclosing rhymes (une rime embrassée)

The rhyme scheme is abba

example: Comment renoncerais-je à tant de souvenirs
Quand l'esprit encombré d'invisibles bagages
Je suis plus affairé dans la mort qu'en voyage
Et je flotte au lieu de sombrer dans le mourir.

Supervielle: "Perdu parmi les
pas . . ."

4.3. Alternate rhymes (une rime croisée)

The rhyme scheme is abab

example: Et une auberge où tout le monde fume
On ne voit plus rien les gens s'entassent
Reconnais-tu cet homme à son chapeau à
plumes
Personne n'est venu pour voir ce qui se passe

Reverdy: *Cabaret*

Feminine and Masculine Rhymes

5.1. Feminine rhymes (une rime féminine)

Feminine rhymes end in a mute *e*.

example: Me font rire, pleurer et rire,
Parler sans avoir rien à dire.

Eluard: *L'Amoureuse*

5.2. Masculine rhymes (une rime masculine)

Masculine rhymes end on a tonic syllable.

example: Et la voilà qui s'échappe des rangs,
Et court! ô mon Dieu, qu'est-ce qu'il lui
prend?

Laforgue: *Dimanches*

It is customary, in traditional prosody, to alternate feminine and masculine rhymes.

Major and Minor Pauses

6.1. The caesura (une césure) in a decasyllabic line

In a ten-syllable line, the caesura generally comes after the fourth syllable.

> example: Tout en chantant/sur le mode mineur
>
> > Verlaine: *Clair de lune*

6.2. The caesura in an alexandrine

In a twelve-syllable line, the caesura comes after the sixth syllable.

> example: Avec ses vêtements/ondoyants et nacrés,
>
> > Baudelaire: "Avec ses vête-
> > > ments . . ."

6.3. The hemistiche (un hémistiche)

In a traditional alexandrine, the caesura divides the line into equal parts called hemistiches. They can frequently be analyzed as autonomous sections. In the following example, the syllabic division within each hemistiche is perfectly symmetrical.

> $$1 \quad 2 \quad 3 \quad 4 \quad 5 \quad 6 \Big/ 7 \quad 8 \quad 9 \ 10 \ 11 \ 12$$
> example: Donner/un sens plus pur/aux mots/de la tribu
> (first hemistiche)   (second hemistiche)
>
> > Mallarmé: *Le Tombeau d'Edgar Poe*

6.4. The pause (une coupe)

The pause occurs within the hemistiche and may become more important than the caesura as the latter is weakened.

> example: Ma Douleur, donne-moi la main; viens par
> ici,
>
> Baudelaire: *Recueillement*

6.5. The weakening of the caesura

The classical alexandrine is a tetrametrical line: it has four symmetrical measures that assure its cadence (see 6.3.). However, as a means of dislocating this predictable structure, poets have introduced a trimetrical line: three pauses instead of the classical four (see 6.4.).

The Run-On Line

7.1. Enjambment (un enjambement)

In traditional poetry, the end of a line corresponded to the syntactical conclusion of a thought. It was then normal to pause at that moment. The enjambment breaks this system by carrying the syntactical sense onto the following line.

> example: De l'éternel azur la sereine ironie
>   Accable, belle indolemment comme les fleurs,
>
> Mallarmé: *L'Azur*

The effect of this practice is to isolate the run-on word or words in the following line. If the word has few syllables, the effect will be to break the rhythmic flow; if, on the contrary, the words occupy the whole hemistiche, then the regular rhythm will be attenuated and a more flowing effect achieved.

7.2 The run-on (un rejet)

That part of the enjambment that runs on to the following line is technically known in French as a *rejet.*

Grouping Lines: Forms

8.1. Stanzas (une strophe)

Rhyme groups occur in twos, threes, fours, or other combinations that together form a stanza. When the group consists of similarly structured lines, the stanza is said to be isometrical (isométrique); when it consists of dissimilar lines, it is said to be heterometrical (hétérométrique).

8.2. The distich (un distique)

The distich is a group of two lines with a complete syntactical meaning.

> example: Que je te dise seulement que depuis des nuits
> je pleure,
> Et que mes sœurs ont bien peur que je n'en
> meure.
>
> Laforgue: "Oh! qu'une, d'Elle-
> même . . ."

8.3. The tercet (un tercet)

The tercet is a group of three lines, borrowed from the Italian *terza rima.*
The last two stanzas of a sonnet are composed of tercets.

> example: Il me faut, vos yeux! Dès que je perds leur
> étoile,
> Le mal des calmes plats s'engouffre dans ma
> voile,

> Le frisson du *Vae soli!* gargouille en mes moel-
> les . . .

Laforgue: Pierrots

8.4. The quatrain (un quatrain)

The quatrain is a group of four lines. It is a very common stanza and can vary its syllabic count.

> example: L'ombre des arbres dans la rivière embrumée
>   Meurt comme de la fumée,
>   Tandis qu'en l'air, parmi les ramures réelles,
>   Se plaignent les tourterelles.

Verlaine: "L'ombre des
arbres . . ."

8.5. Other combinations

A single line: *un monostique;* five lines: *un quintain* or *un quintil;* six lines: *un sixain:* eight lines: *un huitain;* ten lines: *un dizain.*

The Fixed Form Poem

9.1. The sonnet (un sonnet)

Borrowed from the Italians during the French Renaissance, it has become the most popular French poetic form. Known as the Petrarchan sonnet, it is composed of two quatrains and two tercets. The two quatrains follow the enclosing rhyme scheme: abba; the two tercets are composed of couplets (rimes plates), followed by alternate rhymes (rimes croisées): ccdede.

The first two quatrains usually develop the concept and the two tercets represent either a contrast or a parallel. The last

line is frequently called a *vers de chute* since it concludes the sonnet with particular emphasis.

Versification

10.1. Free verse (un vers libre)

Invented by Gustave Kahn (1859–1936), a member of the Symbolist group, free verse is a highly flexible concept. It may signify the absence of a syllabic count, or rhymes, or internal accents, or all three at the same time. It is particularly favored by contemporary poets.

> example: L'empailleur s'était assis
> devant les gorges roses
>
> Follain: *L'Empailleur d'oiseaux*

10.2. The verse line with neither rhyme nor fixed measures

Breaking with traditional restrictions, considered as either too facile or too artificial, contemporary poets have increasingly breached the gap between accented prose and verse, thereby giving rise to a new poetics.

> example: Je me propose, sans être ému, de déclamer à grande voix la strophe sérieuse et froide que vous allez entendre.
>
> Lautréamont: "Chant premier"

10.3. Typography and punctuation

In lieu of fixed poetic forms, the modern poem substitutes a sophisticated visualization dating back to Mallarmé's *Un Coup de dés*. On the page, the words are now disposed according to

emphasis, isolated to signal their importance. Furthermore, through a use of capitals, lower cases, italics, the visual presentation is enhanced. Finally, after Apollinaire, punctuation sometimes disappears entirely from modern poetry.

> example: Sur chaque ardoise
> > qui glissait du toit
> > > on
> > avait écrit
> > > > un poème

> Reverdy: *Les Ardoises du toit*

10.4. The place of accented syllables in the modern poem

With the disappearance of the fixed line, accents no longer occur in a predictable fashion. They are now underlined either through the run-on line (see 7.1.) or through anaphoric constructions (see "Figures of Speech," 1.4.).

10.5. The prose poem (un poème en prose)

Aloysius Bertrand (1807–41), author of a prose poem *Gaspard de la nuit* and Charles Baudelaire (1821–67), author of *Petits Poèmes en prose,* as well as Lautréamont and Rimbaud, pioneered this new form which combines the rhythmic elements of poetry with the tangible distribution of accents and melodic groups found in prose when it is *meant* to be poetic. The intention is thus the key element in distinguishing a prose text from a prose poem.

> example: Des ciels gris de cristal. Un bizarre dessin de ponts, ceux-ci droits, ceux-là bombés, d'autres descendant ou obliquant en angles sur les premiers, et ces figures se renouvelant

dans les autres circuits éclairés du canal, mais tous tellement longs et légers que les rives, chargées de dômes, s'abaissent et s'amoin-drissent.

Rimbaud: *Les Ponts*

S.G.

Figures of Speech

Definition

Until the 1870's in France, rhetoric was taught in the *lycées;* thereafter, though the *classe de rhétorique* no longer corresponded to that program, the art of writing and speaking has remained one of the foundations of a French education. This art was encouraged through such exercises as the *version:* translation from Latin to French, as well as by the *thème:* translation from French to Latin, as well as frequent oral exercises that applied the classic rules of eloquence, formulated by such authorities as Quintilian, whose *Institutio Oratoria* represented one of the fundamental treatises on rhetoric from the Middle Ages forward. His definition of a Figure is still pertinent today as stylisticians study anew the structure of language: "A *figure* . . . as is clear from the name itself, is the term employed when we give our language a conformation other than the obvious and ordinary." The *Institutio Oratoria of Quintilian*, with an English translation by H. E. Butler (New York: Putnam's Sons, 1922), III, 351.

Such was Quintilian's influence that the last of the great French rhetoricians, Pierre Fontanier, when he defined figures of speech, merely reworked the classic presentation: "The figures of speech are the traits, the forms or the turns more or less evident and of a more or less happy effect, through which discourse, in its expression of ideas, thoughts, and feelings, assumes a certain distance from what would have otherwise been a simple and ordinary expression." *Les Figures du discours* (Paris: Flammarion, 1968), p. 64.

Schemes (un schéma)

1.1. Definition

A scheme (Greek *schema*, form, shape) implies a deviation from the ordinary pattern or arrangement of words. The following are some of the most useful found in the poems included in this anthology.

1.2. Alliteration (une allitération)

Repetition of initial or medial consonants in two or more adjacent words.

> example:
> > Vue la disproportion des pépins à la pulpe les oiseaux les apprécient peu, si peu de chose au fond leur reste quand du bec à l'anus ils en sont traversés.

> > Ponge: *Les Mûres*

1.3. Anacoluthon (une anacoluthe)

Construction involving a break in grammatical sequence letting a word be understood where it does not exist.

> example: . . feignant de n'en pas croire mes yeux,
> > J'aurai un: Ah ça, mais, nous avions De Quoi vivre!

> > Laforgue: *Autre Complainte*

Under normal circumstances, there should be a noun after the indefinite article: *un*.

1.4. Anaphora (une anaphore)

Repetition of the same word or groups of words at the beginning of successive verses, clauses, or sentences.

example: Un jour.
Un jour, bientôt peut-être.
Un jour j'arracherai l'ancre qui tient mon na-
vire loin des mers.

Michaux: *Clown*

1.5. Anastrophe (une anastrophe)

Reversing the usual word order.

example: Et que tristes pleuraient, dans les hautes feuil-
lées,
Tes espérances noyées!

Verlaine: "L'ombre des
arbres . . ."

Under normal circumstances, the subject would have preceded
the verb.

1.6. Antithesis (une antithèse)

Positioning of one clause or other member of a sentence
against another to which it is opposed. This juxtapositioning
is often parallel in structure, and can refer to two objects or to
two aspects of the same object.

example: Fuyant, les yeux fermés, je le sens qui regarde

Mallarmé: *L'Azur*

1.7. Apposition (une apposition)

The placing side by side of two coordinate elements, the sec-
ond of which serves as an explanation or modification of the
first. They are most frequently separated by a comma.

example: Vieil océan, ta forme harmonieusement
sphérique, qui réjouit la face grave de la

géométrie, ne me rappelle que trop les petits
yeux de l'homme, pareils à ceux du sanglier
pour la petitesse, et à ceux des oiseaux de nuit
pour la perfection circulaire du contour.

Lautréamont, "Chant premier"

1.8. Asyndeton (une asyndète)

Omission of conjunctions between a series of related clauses.

example: O la face cendrée, l'écusson de crin, les bras
de cristal!

Rimbaud: *Being Beauteous*

1.9. Ellipse (une ellipse)

Omission from a line of one or more words which would complete or clarify the sense, but which are not indispensable for the understanding of the sentence.

example: Qu'y a-t-il derrière
Un mur
des voix

Reverdy: *Route*

The construction *il y a* may precede either *Un mur* or *des voix* or both.

1.10. Epistrophe (une épistrophe)

Repetition of the same word or groups of words at the end of successive clauses or stanzas.

example: Je te salue, vieil océan!

Lautréamont: "Chant premier"

This salutation is repeated at the end of stanzas 2–11.

1.11. Parenthesis (une parenthèse)

Insertion of a complete and isolated verbal unit that interrupts the normal syntactical flow without otherwise affecting it.

> example: Seulement pour qu'enfin
> —car il s'éloigne, n'occupant
> plus que partiellement l'horizon
> bas où il fulgure encore—
> Parant au plus urgent, allant au plus pressé,
> Nous sortions de ces bois,
>
> Ponge: *Le Pré*

1.12. Pleonasm (un pléonasme)

Redundant word or expression which accentuates the meaning of the initial thought.

> example: Et qui dort son sommeil sous une humble pelouse,
>
> Baudelaire: "La servante au grand cœur . . ."

Sommeil repeats the sense of the verb. It is also a metonymy (see 2.6.), standing for death.

Tropes (un trope)

2.1. Definition

A trope (Greek *Trópes,* to turn, or a manner) is any turn away from the normative meaning of a word.

2.2. Hyperbole (une hyperbole)

An exaggerated statement which either by over- or under-emphasis suggests a truth not necessarily literal.

> example: Les étoiles ont cessé de briller
>   La terre ne tourne plus

>   Reverdy: *Son de cloche*

2.3. Irony (une ironie)

A statement that implies the opposite of what it says.

> example: C'est gai,
>   Cette vie;
>   Hein, ma mie,
>   O gué?

>   Laforgue: *Complainte de l'oubli des morts*

2.4. Litotes (une litote)

A statement that says less in order to convey more.

> example: Ah! que la vie est quotidienne . . .

>   Laforgue: *Complainte sur certains ennuis*

2.5. Metaphor (une métaphore)

A transference of meaning from one thing to another by an implied resemblance.

> example: Les cheveux balayant la nuit

>   Reverdy: *Son de cloche*

2.6. Metonymy (une métonymie)

Substituting an attributive word for what is actually meant:

> example: Votre *âme* est un paysage choisi
>
> > Verlaine: *Clair de lune*

âme is substituted for the loved one.

> example: La *Renaissance* résiste
> > dans le clair-obscur des musées
>
> > > Follain: *La Pomme rouge*

Renaissance is substituted for the painters of that period.

2.7. Onomatopoeia (une onomatopée)

A word that imitates the sound of the object described.

> example: Les houles, en roulant les images des cieux
>
> > Baudelaire: *La Vie antérieure*

2.8 Oxymoron (un oxymore)

An alliance of words that are ordinarily contradictory.

> example: "Jouons au plus fidèle!" —A quoi bon, ô Na-
> > ture!"
> > "Autant à qui *perd gagne!*
>
> > Laforgue: *Autre complainte*

2.9. Paranomasia (un paronomase)

The bringing together of words whose sounds are similar but whose meanings are completely different.

example: Mais, chez qui du rêve se dore
Tristement dort une mandore

Mallarmé: "Une dentelle
s'abolit . . ."

2.10. Periphrasis or autonomasia (une autonomase)

A circumlocution whereby a descriptive word or phrase is substituted for a proper name or a proper name is substituted for a quality associated with it.

example: Montrez-moi cet homme de toujours si doux
Qui disait les doigts font monter la terre.

Eluard: *A Pablo Picasso*

2.11. Prosopopoeia (une prosopopée)

Personification of inanimate objects, dead persons, or absent ones, by attributing to them human qualities and abilities (a voice, feelings).

example: O soleil c'est le temps de la Raison ardente
Et j'attends
Pour la suivre toujours la forme noble et douce
Qu'elle prend afin que je l'aime seulement

Apollinaire: *La Jolie Rousse*

2.12. Simile (une comparaison, une analogie)

The transference of meaning from one thing to another by an implied resemblance using like or as (comme).

example: Ta grandeur morale, l'image de l'infini, est immense comme la réflexion du philosophe,

> comme l'amour de la femme, comme la beauté
> divine de l'oiseau, comme les méditations du
> poète.

> Lautréamont: "Chant premier"

2.13. Synecdoche (une synecdoque)

Substituting the general for the specific:

> example: Puisqu'une fois boutonné tout bleu confondu
> dans le ciel je deviens invisible

> Apollinaire: *Poème à Madeleine*

bleu stands for the uniform.

Substituting the specific for the general:

> example: Prendre un tube de vert, l'étaler sur la page,
> Ce n'est pas faire un pré.

> Ponge: *Le Pré*

un tube de vert stands for paint.

                                                        S.G.

A Note on English and French Prosody

English metrical systems are based on the alternation of accented and unaccented syllables, with the number of accented syllables being the basic definition of the verse. *Iambic pentameter*, for example, means that each accented syllable is preceded by an unaccented one, and that the accented syllables are five in number. French verse is identified simply by the number of syllables the line contains, since the *only* accentuation falls on the final pronounced syllable of a phrase. This is the most important difference between English and French prosody, and may be illustrated by two ten-syllable lines.

Tout en chan*tant* sur le mode min*eur*

A *li*ttle *on*ward *lend* thy *gui*ding *hand.*

The more detailed metrical pattern of English permits greater freedom without loss of a unifying rhythm. Readings which distort the normal accentuation of words in order to make them fit a supposed pattern are ruinous. In the line:

The proper study of Mankind is Man

there should not be more than the slightest stress on "of." The deviation from the iambic pattern serves to emphasize "Mankind" which should be read with two accented syllables.

Even the fixed number of accented syllables can be variable. The expected rhythm is so strongly built into the verse that it can serve as a silent counterpoint to lines which in themselves depart from it widely:

O, it came o'er the ear like the sweet sound
That breathes upon a bank of violets
Stealing and giving odor. Enough, no more;

Even without Shakespearean skill it is possible to soften the characteristic rhythms of English enough to suggest the cadences of French. In translating lines of less than ten syllables, one may simply reproduce the number of syllables per line without regard for accentuation. The result is sufficiently strong in rhythm to be acceptable to the ear accustomed to English, and closer in its effect to the French text than would be a normal English meter. French ten-syllable lines may be approximated by introducing a noticeable pause after either the fourth or the sixth syllable. The *alexandrine* is more difficult. Verses over ten or eleven syllables in length tend to have six accented syllables in English, and experiments in such meters have been few and unconvincing, witness *Evangeline*. This does not mean that the translator of a twelve-syllable line is restricted to ten syllables, but that he is limited to five accented ones. Alexander Pope's illustration offers comment enough:

A needless Alexandrine ends the song,
That, like a wounded snake, drags its slow
    length along.

                                                              P.T.

The Poems

Charles Baudelaire ✣✣✣ 1821-67

Simile is to metaphor as comparison is to transformation. When Baudelaire writes, "You are a sky of autumn, fair and rose!" he is making a gesture of faith in the power of language to accomplish something that cannot be achieved through any other means. The metaphor is an act. Outside the experience of the poet, which may itself be wholly or partially verbal, the woman and the sky are united only in the line of verse. Emphasis on metaphor has been fundamental to post-Parnassian poetics, together with a belief that human experience, transformed by art, can be not only communicated but to some extent redeemed.

Baudelaire sees the artist, by virtue of his superior vision, as isolated in a hostile society: "with his giant wings he cannot walk the ground." While his acute but unsentimental feeling of estrangement may strike us as modern, it is also related to a more comforting Romantic concept of individualism. Later poets will be dominated by a sense of the Absurd, convinced that human values, aesthetic or otherwise, correspond to nothing outside the human sphere. Mallarmé's *Azur* is non-being; its absolute blankness has little in common with the implacable eyes of Beauty which, however inhuman, still *has* eyes, and is still a goal. In Baudelaire's view, man and the universe interact as they will not in later writers. Nature is a forest of symbols which are observing us even as we look at them. Underlying the mysterious façades of the world is a shadowy unity in which thoughts and sensations merge in lulling peace. This is not a Nirvana, since, incomplete in itself, it seeks and finds an equivalent in words, among them those of "La Vie antérieure."

P.T.

La Vie antérieure

J'ai longtemps habité sous de vastes portiques
Que les soleils marins teignaient de mille feux,
Et que leurs grands piliers, droits et majestueux,
Rendaient pareils, le soir, aux grottes basaltiques.

Les houles, en roulant les images des cieux,
Mêlaient d'une façon solennelle et mystique
Les tout-puissants accords de leur riche musique
Aux couleurs du couchant reflété par mes yeux.

C'est là que j'ai vécu dans les voluptés calmes,
Au milieu de l'azur, des vagues, des splendeurs
Et des esclaves nus, tout imprégnés d'odeurs,

Qui me rafraîchissaient le front avec des palmes,
Et dont l'unique soin était d'approfondir
Le secret douloureux qui me faisait languir.

Les Fleurs du mal

La Cloche fêlée

Il est amer et doux, pendant les nuits d'hiver,
D'écouter, près du feu qui palpite et qui fume,

Preceding Life

Once I lived beneath vast porticos
Marine suns colored with a thousand fires,
And whose tall columns, straight majestic spires,
Made them, at twilight, seem volcanic grottos.

The sea-swell, surging mirror of the skies,
Gravely and mysteriously wound
With opulent music, overwhelming sound,
The sunset hues reflected in my eyes.

Long my home was that voluptuous calm,
Among the blue, the splendors, tranquil waves,
And, all steeped in fragrance, naked slaves

To cool my forehead, wafting fans of palm,
Only concerned to probe, with studious care,
The bitter secret that made me languish there.

                                              P.T.

The Flawed Bell

It is bitter and pleasant to spend a winter night
Close to the pulsating, smoking fire and listen

Les souvenirs lointains lentement s'élever
Au bruit des carillons qui chantent dans la brume.

Bienheureuse la cloche au gosier vigoureux,
Qui, malgré sa vieillesse, alerte et bien portante,
Jette fidèlement son cri religieux,
Ainsi qu'un vieux soldat qui veille sous la tente!

Moi, mon âme est fêlée, et lorsqu'en ses ennuis
Elle veut de ses chants peupler l'air froid des nuits,
Il arrive souvent que sa voix affaiblie

Semble le râle épais d'un blessé qu'on oublie
Au bord d'un lac de sang, sous un grand tas de morts,
Et qui meurt, sans bouger, dans d'immenses efforts.

Les Fleurs du mal

Recueillement

Sois sage, ô ma Douleur, et tiens-toi plus tranquille.
Tu réclamais le Soir; il descend; le voici:
Une atmosphère obscure enveloppe la ville,
Aux uns portant la paix, aux autres le souci.

Pendant que des mortels la multitude vile,
Sous le fouet du Plaisir, ce bourreau sans merci,
Va cueillir des remords dans la fête servile,
Ma Douleur, donne-moi la main; viens par ici,

Loin d'eux. Vois se pencher les défuntes Années,

As distant memories indolently rise
To the sound of carillons singing in the mist.

Happy the bell whose energetic throat,
Old but with its keen vigor yet unspent,
Faithful to its pious charge cries out
Like an old soldier on watch inside his tent.

As for me, my soul is flawed, and its despair,
Trying with songs to people the night's cold air,
Often finds its weakened voice to have the sound

Of a wounded man's thick breathing, as he dies
Near a lake of blood, forgotten, held to the ground
By the heaped-up dead, immobile and struggling to rise.

                                                        P.T.

Meditation

Be good, my Sorrow, try to be calmer. See,
You couldn't wait for Evening; it is here.
Now shadows are enveloping the city,
Offering peace to some, to others fear.

Let the vile multitudes of human beast
That the hangman, Pleasure, scourges with no pity,
Accumulate remorse at the servile feast—
My Sorrow, give me your hand, come with me

Far from them all. Watch the dead Years pose

Sur les balcons du ciel, en robes surannées;
Surgir du fond des eaux le Regret souriant;

Le Soleil moribond s'endormir sous une arche,
Et, comme un long linceul traînant à l'Orient,
Entends, ma chère, entends la douce Nuit qui marche.

Les Fleurs du mal

La Beauté

Je suis belle, ô mortels! comme un rêve de pierre,
Et mon sein, où chacun s'est meurtri tour à tour,
Est fait pour inspirer au poëte un amour
Eternel et muet ainsi que la matière.

Je trône dans l'azur comme un sphinx incompris;
J'unis un cœur de neige à la blancheur des cygnes;
Je hais le mouvement qui déplace les lignes,
Et jamais je ne pleure et jamais je ne ris.

Les poëtes, devant mes grandes attitudes,
Que j'ai l'air d'emprunter aux plus fiers monuments,
Consumeront leurs jours en d'austères études;

Car j'ai, pour fasciner ces dociles amants,
De purs miroirs qui font toutes choses plus belles:
Mes yeux, mes larges yeux aux clartés éternelles!

Les Fleurs du mal

On balconies of the sky, in old-fashioned clothes,
Smiling Regret from boundless waters rise,

The dying Sun fall asleep beneath an arch;
And, like a long shroud flowing from eastern skies,
Listen, my dear one, listen to gentle Night's soft march.

                                                    P.T.

Beauty

My beauty, O mortals! is a dream of stone,
And my breast, whose bruising hardness you have known,
Is made to inspire poets with a love
Perpetual as matter, mute as bone.

Like an enigmatic sphinx I rule the sky;
To the whiteness of swans I add a heart of snow;
I hate the movement that distorts the line;
And never do I laugh, and never cry.

Poets confronting my august displays,
Modelled, it seems, on monuments of state,
To austere studies sacrifice their days,

Meek lovers my pure mirrors fascinate,
Making all things more beautiful in their sight,
My great clear eyes of everlasting light.

                                                    P.T.

Avec ses vêtements ondoyants et nacrés,
Même quand elle marche on croirait qu'elle danse,
Comme ces longs serpents que les jongleurs sacrés
Au bout de leurs bâtons agitent en cadence.

Comme le sable morne et l'azur des déserts,
Insensibles tous deux à l'humaine souffrance,
Comme les longs réseaux de la houle des mers,
Elle se développe avec indifférence.

Ses yeux polis sont faits de minéraux charmants,
Et dans cette nature étrange et symbolique
Où l'ange inviolé se mêle au sphinx antique,

Où tout n'est qu'or, acier, lumière et diamants,
Resplendit à jamais, comme un astre inutile,
La froide majesté de la femme stérile.

Les Fleurs du mal

Causerie

Vous êtes un beau ciel d'automne, clair et rose!
Mais la tristesse en moi monte comme la mer,
Et laisse, en refluant, sur ma lèvre morose
Le souvenir cuisant de son limon amer.

In her clothes of undulating pearl,
When she only walks, she seems to be dancing,
Like those long snakes holy fakirs unfurl
From the end of sticks, rhythmically advancing.

Like the bleak sand of deserts and their skies,
Blind to the torments of the human race,
Like the endless links that bind the swelling tides,
Her pure indifference deploys her grace.

Her polished eyes are minerals that charm,
And her nature, emblematic and bizarre,
Where inviolate angel blends with the sphinx of old,

Where all is steel, light, diamonds, and gold,
Enshrines forever, like a useless star,
The sterile woman's gleaming realm of cold.

P.T.

A Little Talk

You are a sky of autumn, fair and rose!
But my native sadness rises like the sea,
And falling, on my sullen lips bestows
A bitter silt of caustic memory.

—Ta main se glisse en vain sur mon sein qui se pâme;
Ce qu'elle cherche, amie, est un lieu saccagé
Par la griffe et la dent féroce de la femme.
Ne cherchez plus mon cœur; les bêtes l'ont mangé.

Mon cœur est un palais flétri par la cohue;
On s'y soûle, on s'y tue, on s'y prend aux cheveux!
—Un parfum nage autour de votre gorge nue! . . .

O Beauté, dur fléau des âmes, tu le veux!
Avec tes yeux de feu, brillants comme des fêtes,
Calcine ces lambeaux qu'ont épargnés les bêtes!

Les Fleurs du mal

La servante au grand cœur dont vous étiez jalouse,
Et qui dort son sommeil sous une humble pelouse,
Nous devrions pourtant lui porter quelques fleurs.
Les morts, les pauvres morts, ont de grandes douleurs,
Et quand Octobre souffle, émondeur des vieux arbres,
Son vent mélancolique à l'entour de leurs marbres,
Certe, ils doivent trouver les vivants bien ingrats,
A dormir, comme ils font, chaudement dans leurs draps,
Tandis que, dévorés de noires songeries,
Sans compagnon de lit, sans bonnes causeries,
Vieux squelettes gelés travaillés par le ver,
Ils sentent s'égoutter les neiges de l'hiver
Et le siècle couler, sans qu'amis ni famille
Remplacent les lambeaux qui pendent à leur grille.

Your gliding hand may hold my chest enthralled,
But its quest leads to a ruin, torn apart
By the feral teeth of women, by their claws;
The beasts of prey have fed upon my heart.

My heart is a palace where a blind horde gloats,
A place of murder, drunkenness and strife!
Above your naked breast a perfume floats! . . .

O Beauty, scourge of souls, I will obey!
With your eyes, in brilliant festivals of fire,
Consume these fragments spared by the beasts of prey!
                                                  P.T.

My old nurse whose kind heart made you jealous
And who sleeps her sleep beneath a humble lawn,
We really ought to bring her a few flowers.
The dead, poor things, the dead have bitter sorrows,
And when October, coming to prune old trees,
Wraps their tombs with melancholy wind,
How selfish they must think the living are
For sleeping under blankets, soft and warm,
While they, devoured by black reveries,
With no one to talk to, no one to share their bed,
Old frozen bones the worms have fretted thin,
Feel drop by drop the winter snows give way,
And decades flow by, while family and friends
Leave tattered rags to decorate their graves.

Lorsque la bûche siffle et chante, si le soir,
Calme, dans le fauteuil je la voyais s'asseoir,
Si, par une nuit bleue et froide de décembre,
Je la trouvais tapie en un coin de ma chambre,
Grave, et venant du fond de son lit éternel
Couver l'enfant grandi de son œil maternel,
Que pourrais-je répondre à cette âme pieuse,
Voyant tomber des pleurs de sa paupière creuse?

Les Fleurs du mal

Charles Baudelaire

When logs in the evening fireplace crack and sing,
If I saw her sit down calmly in her chair,
If, on a blue and cold December night,
She huddled in a corner of my room,
Unsmiling, come from her eternal bed
To brood, with a mother's gaze, her grown-up child,
What answer could I give that pious soul,
Seeing her empty eyelids wet with tears?

                                        P.T.

Stéphane Mallarmé ✠✠✠ 1842-98

Poetry in France has traditionally recognized the validity of at least two distinct poetic styles. The first, and most favored, considers the message as preeminent, the execution meant to facilitate its readability. The second concentrates on the perfect accomplishment of a hermetic thought; language, metrics, and stanzaic structure tend to be complex. Stéphane Mallarmé began writing elegies in the manner of Lamartine, borrowing from that Romantic poet the theme of the inaccessibility of the idea of which the *fenêtre* becomes the main symbol. In these early poems, the message was easily understood: the poet, in his painful isolation, had to suffer the vulgarity and meaninglessness of a material world. Yet hope, often conditional, remained that he might still escape this plight. Mallarmé slowly internalized this conflict and substituted his own inability to render the poetic potential of the universe in its totality, the difficulty of creation, for the obstacles previously erected by the world.

The internal struggle was further purified in his later work, especially in his long poem *Un Coup de dés jamais n' abolira le hasard*. Here, according to one interpretation, Mallarmé proposed a new poetic language characterized by an arcane syntactical structure, elliptical associations, and elusive metaphors. The purity that he sought to translate was akin to that of music: words had to convey the phonemic element giving them the quality of a musical note. This factor became as significant as the transmission of the message itself. The result was the formulation of one of the most hermetic forms of poetic language. The rigor that Mallarmé imposed upon himself others were to appreciate, recognizing in that nineteenth-century poet one of the major precursors of modern poetry.

S.G.

L'*Azur*

De l'éternel azur la sereine ironie
Accable, belle indolemment comme les fleurs,
Le poëte impuissant qui maudit son génie
A travers un désert stérile de Douleurs.

Fuyant, les yeux fermés, je le sens qui regarde
Avec l'intensité d'un remords atterrant,
Mon âme vide. Où fuir? Et quelle nuit hagarde
Jeter, lambeaux, jeter sur ce mépris navrant?

Brouillards, montez! Versez vos cendres monotones
Avec de longs haillons de brume dans les cieux
Qui noiera le marais livide des automnes
Et bâtissez un grand plafond silencieux!

Et toi, sors des étangs léthéens et ramasse
En t'en venant la vase et les pâles roseaux,
Cher Ennui, pour boucher d'une main jamais lasse
Les grands trous bleus que font méchamment les oiseaux.

Encor! que sans répit les tristes cheminées
Fument, et que de suie une errante prison
Éteigne dans l'horreur de ses noires traînnées
Le soleil se mourant jaunâtre à l'horizon!

—Le Ciel est mort. —Vers toi, j'accours! donne, ô matière,
L'oubli de l'Idéal cruel et du Péché
A ce martyr qui vient partager la litière
Où le bétail heureux des hommes est couché,

The Sky

The tranquil irony of the eternal sky,
Indolently beautiful like flowers,
Crushes the impotent poet, cursing his gift
Across a sterile wilderness of Sorrows.

Escaping, my eyes closed, I feel its glance piercing
With the intensity of a crushing remorse
My empty soul. Where can I flee? And what haggard
Rags of night can I cast on this devastating scorn?

Mists arise! Pour out your monotonous ashes
In endless shreds of haze across the heavens
That will drown the livid marshes of autumns
And fashion a measureless and silent ceiling!

And you, leave the Lethean swamps and gather
Upon your journey the slime and the pallid reeds,
Dear Ennui, to fill with a never-wearied hand
The great blue holes spitefully made by birds.

Further, let the melancholy chimneys smoke
Ceaselessly, and a wandering prison of soot
Suffocate in the horror of its black trails
The yellowing sun that dies on the horizon!

—The Heavens are dead.—I rush toward you! O matter,
Grant that the cruel Ideal and Sin be forgotten
By this martyr who has come to share the stable
With the herds of men, contented cattle, at rest,

Car j'y veux, puisque enfin ma cervelle, vidée
Comme le pot de fard gisant au pied du mur,
N'a plus l'art d'attifer la sanglotante idée,
Lugubrement bâiller vers un trépas obscur . . .

En vain! l'Azur triomphe, et je l'entends qui chante
Dans les cloches. Mon âme, il se fait voix pour plus
Nous faire peur avec sa victoire méchante,
Et du métal vivant sort en bleus angélus!

Il roule par la brume, ancien et traverse
Ta native agonie ainsi qu'un glaive sûr;
Où fuir dans la révolte inutile et perverse?
Je suis hanté. L'Azur! l'Azur! l'Azur! l'Azur!

> *Du Parnasse contemporain*

Brise marine

La chair est triste, hélas! et j'ai lu tous les livres.
Fuir! là-bas fuir! Je sens que des oiseaux sont ivres
D'être parmi l'écume inconnue et les cieux!
Rien, ni les vieux jardins reflétés par les yeux
Ne retiendra ce cœur qui dans la mer se trempe
O nuits! ni la clarté déserte de ma lampe
Sur le vide papier que la blancheur défend
Et ni la jeune femme allaitant son enfant.
Je partirai! Steamer balançant ta mâture,
Lève l'ancre pour une exotique nature!

Un Ennui, désolé par les cruels espoirs,
Croit encore à l'adieu suprême des mouchoirs!

For that is my wish, since my brain, at last, emptied
Like an empty cosmetic jar against a wall,
Can no longer decorate the sobbing idea,
Lugubriously to yawn toward a humble death . . .

In vain! The Sky triumphs, and I hear its bells
Singing. Listen, my soul, it becomes a voice
To frighten us more with its spiteful victory,
Angelus tolling blue from the living metal!

Ancient it rolls through the mists and penetrates
Your native agony like a faithful sword;
Where can I flee in this useless perverse revolt?
I am possessed. The Sky! The Sky! The Sky! The Sky!

                                                    S.G.

Sea Breeze

The flesh is weary, alas! And I've read all there is.
To flee! To flee out there! I feel that birds are drunk
From being amid the unknown foam and skies!
Nothing, neither old gardens reflected in my eyes
Will hold back this heart that drenches itself in the sea
O nights! nor the desert brightness of my lamp
On the empty paper its whiteness defends,
And not even that young woman nursing her child.
I will go! Steamer, balancing your masts,
Weigh anchor for exotic lands!

An Ennui, now afflicted by cruel hopes,
Trusts the supreme farewell of handkerchiefs!

Et, peut-être, les mâts, invitant les orages
Sont-ils de ceux qu'un vent penche sur les naufrages
Perdus, sans mâts, sans mâts, ni fertiles îlots . . .
Mais, ô mon cœur, entends le chant des matelots!

Du Parnasse contemporain

Le Tombeau D'Edgar Poe

Tel qu'en Lui-même enfin l'éternité le change,
Le Poëte suscite avec un glaive nu
Son siècle épouvanté de n'avoir pas connu
Que la mort triomphait dans cette voix étrange!

Eux, comme un vil sursaut d'hydre oyant jadis l'ange
Donner un sens plus pur aux mots de la tribu
Proclamèrent très haut le sortilège bu
Dans le flot sans honneur de quelque noir mélange.

Du sol et de la nue hostiles, ô grief!
Si notre idée avec ne sculpte un bas-relief
Dont la tombe de Poe éblouissante s'orne,

Calme bloc ici bas chu d'un désastre obscur,
Que ce granit du moins montre à jamais sa borne
Aux noirs vols du Blasphème épars dans le futur.

Hommages et tombeaux

And, perhaps, the masts inviting the storms to come,
Are those that are angled by winds over shipwrecks
Lost, without masts, without masts, nor fertile islets . . .
But o my heart, listen! The sailors are singing!

S.G.

The Tomb of Edgar Poe

By Eternity changed at last into Himself,
The Poet arouses with a naked blade
His century terror-stricken not to have known
Death was triumphant in that strange voice!

They, as the vile hydra once writhed to hear the angel
Give a purer meaning to the words of the tribe,
Loudly proclaimed that he had drunk the spell
From the honorless tide of some odious draught.

From hostile earth and heavens, O Grievance!
If our idea cannot chisel a bas-relief
To be an ornament on Poe's resplendent tomb,

Tranquil stone fallen from some dark disaster,
At least may this granite ever mark a limit
To the scattered black flights of Blasphemy to come.

S.G.

Une dentelle s'abolit
Dans le doute du Jeu suprême
À n'entr'ouvrir comme un blasphème
Qu'absence éternelle de lit.

Cet unanime blanc conflit
D'une guirlande avec la même,
Enfui contre la vitre blême
Flotte plus qu'il n'ensevelit.

Mais, chez qui du rêve se dore
Tristement dort une mandore
Au creux néant musicien

Telle que vers quelque fenêtre
Selon nul ventre que le sien,
Filial on aurait pu naître.

Autres poèmes et sonnets

Le vierge, le vivace et le bel aujourd'hui
Va-t-il nous déchirer avec un coup d'aile ivre
Ce lac dur oublié que hante sous le givre
Le transparent glacier des vols qui n'ont pas fui!

The lace curtain effaced
In doubt of the ultimate Wager
Revealing just, o blasphemy,
Eternal absence of bed.

This unanimous white strife
Of a garland with itself,
Fled against the pallid glass,
Hovers more than it enshrouds.

But where he gilds himself with dreams
Sadly sleeps a mandola
With its hollow musical void

Such that toward a window
From no other womb but its own
Filial one might have been born.

                                    S.G.

Will new and alive the beautiful today
Shatter with a blow of drunken wing
This hard lake, forgotten, haunted under rime
By the transparent glacier, flights unflown!

Un cygne d'autrefois se souvient que c'est lui
Magnifique mais qui sans espoir se délivre
Pour n'avoir pas chanté la région où vivre
Quand du stérile hiver a resplendi l'ennui.

Tout son col secouera cette blanche agonie
Par l'espace infligé à l'oiseau qui le nie,
Mais non l'horreur du sol où le plumage est pris.

Fantôme qu'à ce lieu son pur éclat assigne,
Il s'immobilise au songe froid de mépris
Que vêt parmi l'exil inutile le Cygne.

Plusieurs sonnets

Ses purs ongles très haut dédiant leur onyx,
L'Angoisse, ce minuit, soutient, lampadophore,
Maint rêve vespéral brûlé par le Phénix
Que ne recueille pas de cinéraire amphore.

Sur les crédences, au salon vide: nul ptyx,
Aboli bibelot d'inanité sonore,
(Car le Maître est allé puiser des pleurs au Styx
Avec ce seul objet dont le Néant s'honore).

Mais proche la croisée au nord vacante, un or
Agonise selon peut-être le décor
Des licornes ruant du feu contre une nixe,

A swan of long ago remembers now that he,
Magnificent but lost to hope, is doomed
For having failed to sing the realms of life
When the ennui of sterile winter gleamed.

His neck will shake off the white torment space
Inflicts upon the bird for his denial,
But not this horror, plumage trapped in ice.

Phantom by brilliance captive to this place,
Immobile, he assumes disdain's cold dream,
Which, in his useless exile, robes the Swan.

                                   P.T. and M.Z.S.

The onyx of her pure nails offered high,
Lampadephore at midnight, Anguish bears
Many a twilight dream the Phoenix burned
To ashes gathered by no amphora.

On the credence, in the empty room: no ptyx,
Curio of vacuous sonority, extinct
(The Master's gone to dip tears from the Styx
With that unique delight of Nothingness).

But near the vacant northern window, gold
Expires, conformed perhaps to the motif
Of unicorn flames rearing at a nymph,

Elle, défunte nue en le miroir, encor
Que, dans l'oubli fermé par le cadre, se fixe
De scintillations sitôt le septuor.

Plusieurs sonnets

L'Après-Midi d'un Faune

Églogue

Le Faune

Ces nymphes, je les veux perpétuer.

                               Si clair,
Leur incarnat léger, qu'il voltige dans l'air
Assoupi de sommeils touffus.

                        Aimai-je un rêve?
Mon doute, amas de nuit ancienne, s'achève
En maint rameau subtil, qui, demeuré les vrais
Bois mêmes, prouve, hélas! que bien seul je m'offrais
Pour triomphe la faute idéale de roses.
Réfléchissons . . .

               ou si les femmes dont tu gloses
Figurent un souhait de tes sens fabuleux!
Faune, l'illusion s'échappe des yeux bleus
Et froids, comme une source en pleurs, de la plus chaste
Mais, l'autre tout soupirs, dis-tu qu'elle contraste
Comme brise du jour chaude dans ta toison?
Que non! par l'immobile et lasse pâmoison
Suffoquant de chaleurs le matin frais s'il lutte,

She, in the mirror, nude, defunct, although
Within the framed oblivion at once
Appears, all scintillation, the Septet.
                                    P.T. and M.Z.S.

The Afternoon of a Faun

Eclogue

          The Faun
I would perpetuate these nymphs.
                              So clear,
The glow of them, so nimble in the air
Drowsiness encumbers—

                              Did I dream that love?
My doubt, the hoard of ancient night, divides
In subtle branches, which, the only woods
Remaining, prove, alas! that all alone
I triumphed in the ideal fault of roses.
Let's think . . .

                    or if the women you malign
Configurate your fabled senses' wish!
That error flees before the chaste nymph's eyes,
As blue and cold, Faun, as a weeping stream.
But, for the other, would she not compare,
All sighs, to day's warm breezes in your fleece?
No! through this immobile lassitude
That stifles any protest from cool morning,

Ne murmure point d'eau que ne verse ma flûte
Au bosquet arrosé d'accords; et le seul vent
Hors des deux tuyaux prompt à s'exhaler avant
Qu'il disperse le son dans une pluie aride,
C'est, à l'horizon pas remué d'une ride,
Le visible et serein souffle artificiel
De l'inspiration, qui regagne le ciel.

O bords siciliens d'un calme marécage
Qu'à l'envi de soleils ma vanité saccage,
Tacite sous les fleurs d'étincelles, CONTEZ
« *Que je coupais ici les creux roseaux domptés*
» *Par le talent; quand, sur l'or glauque de lointaines*
» *Verdures dédiant leur vigne à des fontaines,*
» *Ondoie une blancheur animale au repos:*
» *Et qu'au prélude lent où naissent les pipeaux*
» *Ce vol de cygnes, non! de naïades se sauve*
» *Ou plonge . . .* »

           Inerte, tout brûle dans l'heure fauve
Sans marquer par quel art ensemble détala
Trop d'hymen souhaité de qui cherche le *la*:
Alors m'éveillerai-je à la ferveur première,
Droit et seul, sous un flot antique de lumière,
Lys! et l'un de vous tous pour l'ingénuité.

Autre que ce doux rien par leur lèvre ébruité,
Le baiser, qui tout bas des perfides assure,
Mon sein, vierge de preuve, atteste une morsure
Mystérieuse, due à quelque auguste dent;
Mais, bast! arcane tel élut pour confident
Le jonc vaste et jumeau dont sous l'azur on joue:
Qui, détournant à soi le trouble de la joue,
Rêve, dans un solo long, que nous amusions

No water murmurs but the harmony
My flute pours on the grove; the only wind,
Quick to exhale from the two pipes, before
It dissipates the sound in arid rain,
Is, on the smooth horizon nothing moves,
The visible, serene, and artificial breath
Of inspiration, homing to the sky.

O you Sicilian shores of a calm marsh,
Which, rivaling suns, my vanity lays waste,
Silent beneath the flowers of light, RELATE
"I was cutting here the hollow reeds by talent
Mastered; against the distant glaucous gold
Of foliage offering its vines to streams,
Undulates animal whiteness in repose;
And, when the pipes are born in slow prelude,
A flight of swans, no! naiads hastens off
Or dives . . ."

                    Inert, all burns in the tawny hour
With no sign of the wiles by which escaped
That nuptial surfeit the musician sought.
Then to my native fervor I'll awake,
Upright, alone in ancient floods of light,
Lilies! and by my innocence your peer.

Save this sweet nothing rumored by their lips,
The kiss, mute witness to their perfidy,
Untouched by any proof, my chest reveals
Mysterious marks of sacramental teeth:
Enough! if such arcana deign to speak,
It is through vast twin reeds played under heaven,
Which, turning to themselves the cheek's emotion,
In an endless solo, dream that we amused

La beauté d'alentour par des confusions
Fausses entre elle-même et notre chant crédule;
Et de faire aussi haut que l'amour se module
Evanouir du songe ordinaire de dos
Ou de flanc pur suivis avec mes regards clos,
Une sonore, vaine et monotone ligne.

Tâche donc, instrument des fuites, ô maligne
Syrinx, de refleurir aux lacs où tu m'attends!
Moi, de ma rumeur fier, je vais parler longtemps
Des déesses; et par d'idolâtres peintures,
A leur ombre enlever encore des ceintures:
Ainsi, quand des raisins j'ai sucé la clarté,
Pour bannir un regret par ma feinte écarté,
Rieur, j'élève au ciel d'été la grappe vide
Et, soufflant dans ses peaux lumineuses, avide
D'ivresse, jusqu'au soir je regarde au travers.

O nymphes, regonflons des souvenirs divers.
«Mon œil, trouant les joncs, dardait chaque encolure
» Immortelle, qui noie en l'onde sa brûlure
» Avec un cri de rage au ciel de la forêt;
» Et le splendide bain de cheveux disparaît
» Dans les clartés et les frissons, ô pierreries!
» J'accours; quand, à mes pieds, s'entrejoignent (meurtries
» De la langueur goûtée à ce mal d'être deux)
» Des dormeuses parmi leurs seuls bras hasardeux;
» Je les ravis, sans les désenlacer, et vole
» A ce massif, haï par l'ombrage frivole,
» De roses tarissant tout parfum au soleil,
» Où notre ébat au jour consumé soit pareil.»
Je t'adore, courroux des vierges, ô délice
Farouche du sacré fardeau nu qui se glisse
Pour fuir ma lèvre en feu buvant, comme un éclair

The beauty here around us, foolishly
Equating it with our own credulous song;
And of abstracting from the banal vision,
Contours of back or breast traced by closed eyes,
As high as love itself can modulate,
A sonorous, futile, uninflected line.

Try, then, malicious Syrinx, instrument
Of flight, to flower anew beside our lakes!
As for me, proud of my voice, I'll speak at length
Of those divinities and by idolatrous
Depictions strip yet more veils from their shade.
Thus, when I've sucked the brightness out of grapes,
To chase regret deflected by my feint,
I lift the empty cluster to the sky,
Laughing, and, wild to be drunk, inflate
The shining skins and look through them till night.

O nymphs, let us inflate our MEMORIES.
"Piercing the reeds, my gaze stabs deathless
Throats, which drown their burning in the wave
With cries of outrage to the forest sky;
The splendid shower of tresses disappears
In a shimmering of precious gems! I lunge;
And there, entangled at my feet (cast down
By languor in the pain of being two)
Lie sleeping nymphs, at risk in their embrace;
I carry them off, still intertwined, and fly
To that high garden frivolous shadow scorns,
Where roses yield their fragrance to the sun
And, like the day, our sport may be consumed."
I love you, wrath of virgins, savage bliss—
The sacred naked burden as it writhes
To flee the fiery lightning of my lips,

Tressaille! la frayeur secrète de la chair:
Des pieds de l'inhumaine au cœur de la timide
Que délaisse à la fois une innocence, humide
De larmes folles ou de moins tristes vapeurs.
«*Mon crime, c'est d'avoir, gai de vaincre ces peurs*
»*Traîtresses, divisé la touffe échevelée*
»*De baisers que les dieux gardaient si bien mêlée:*
»*Car, à peine j'allais cacher un rire ardent*
»*Sous les replis heureux d'une seule (gardant*
»*Par un doigt simple, afin que sa candeur de plume*
»*Se teignît à l'émoi de sa sœur qui s'allume,*
»*La petite, naïve et ne rougissant pas:)*
»*Que de mes bras, défaits par de vagues trépas,*
»*Cette proie, à jamais ingrate se délivre*
»*Sans pitié du sanglot dont j'étais encore ivre.*»

Tant pis! vers le bonheur d'autres m'entraîneront
Par leur tresse nouée aux cornes de mon front:
Tu sais, ma passion, que, pourpre et déjà mûre,
Chaque grenade éclate et d'abeilles murmure;
Et notre sang, épris de qui le va saisir,
Coule pour tout l'essaim éternel du désir.
A l'heure où ce bois d'or et de cendres se teinte
Une fête s'exalte en la feuillée éteinte:
Etna! c'est parmi toi visité de Vénus
Sur ta lave posant ses talons ingénus,
Quand tonne un somme triste ou s'épuise la flamme.
Je tiens la reine!

        O sûr châtiment . . .
                        Non, mais l'âme
De paroles vacante et ce corps alourdi
Tard succombent au fier silence de midi:
Sans plus il faut dormir en l'oubli du blasphème,

While, from the cruel one's feet to the shy one's heart,
I drink the secret terror of the flesh;
And innocence, all moist with frenzied tears
Or with less woeful vapors, quits them both.
"Gay with the conquest of those treacherous fears,
I sinned when I divided that disheveled
Bouquet of kisses mingled by the gods;
For, as I moved to hide an ardent laugh
Deep amid joyous curves, (and only held
By one sole finger, that her sister's kindling
Might lend its color to her downy whiteness,
The little one, unblushing and naive)
Then, from my arms, undone as if by death,
This prey, ungrateful to the end, breaks free,
Spurning the sob that kept me drunken still."

Who cares! their tresses knotted on my horns,
Others will draw me on toward happiness.
You know, my passion, that, crimson now and ripe,
Pomegranates burst in a hum of bees:
Our blood, enamored of its tyrant, flows
For the eternal swarming of desire.
When these woodlands take the hues of ash and gold,
Rejoicing quickens in the darkened leaves:
Etna! in your midst, where Venus comes,
Touching your lava with ingenuous feet,
When thunders sorry sleep or the flame burns dry.
I hold the queen!

                    Sure punishment . . .
                                        No, the soul
Empty of words and this now torpid flesh
To noon's proud silence all too late succumb.
I must forget that blasphemy in sleep,

Sur le sable altéré gisant et comme j'aime
Ouvrir ma bouche à l'astre efficace des vins!

Couple, adieu; je vais voir l'ombre que tu devins.

Autres poèmes

Laid out on thirsty sand, mouth open wide—
Oh, delight!—to wine's effectual star.

Couple, farewell; I'll see the shade that you became.

                                    P.T. and M.Z.S.

Paul Verlaine ✠✠✠ 1844-96

Verlaine's "Art poétique" declares that the most important quality of poetry is music, which is, to begin with, the sound and rhythm of its words. The domain Verlaine prefers is where the precise and the imprecise meet, where a misty greyness softens color to nuance, and where eloquence and wit are disdained in favor of tenderness and dream. "Musical" should be understood in contrast to cerebral; as sound prevails over meaning, so feeling prevails over thought. And feeling itself occurs as an element in the flux, like wind or moonlight or rain, seeming to require neither explanation or cause. The personal experience which prompted the poem is blurred, almost extinguished; the emotions are generalized, impersonal, their imprecision making them more immediately relevant to the reader. Drifting melancholy, sighs for the swiftness of time or the inadequacies of love, acquire a mysterious, floating grace. They seem both attractive and significant. The delicate texture of this verse is unique in French poetry, and is comparable to the shimmering surfaces of Monet or Debussy. When Verlaine later renounced his impressionistic style in a quest for solidarity and clarity, writing *Sagesse,* he demonstrated that sharp outlines may surround nothing, while a network of mist may give new form to the real.

P.T.

Clair de lune

Votre âme est un paysage choisi
Que vont charmant masques et bergamasques,
Jouant du luth, et dansant, et quasi
Tristes sous leurs déguisements fantasques.

Tout en chantant sur le mode mineur
L'amour vainqueur et la vie opportune,
Ils n'ont pas l'air de croire à leur bonheur
Et leur chanson se mêle au clair de lune,

Au calme clair de lune triste et beau,
Qui fait rêver les oiseaux dans les arbres
Et sangloter d'extase les jets d'eau,
Les grands jets d'eau sveltes parmi les marbres.

Fêtes galantes

Le Faune

Un vieux faune de terre cuite
Rit au centre des boulingrins,
Présageant sans doute une suite
Mauvaise à ces instants sereins

Qui m'ont conduit et t'ont conduite,
—Mélancoliques pèlerins,—

Moonlight

To charm the graceful landscape of your soul,
Courtly masks and pantomimes devise
Dances to the lute. They are almost
Sad beneath their whimsical disguise.

Singing always in a minor key
The triumphs that to love and life belong,
They almost seem to waver in their joy,
And the moonlight flows into their song.

The tranquil moonlight, beautiful and sad,
Sets the birds among dark branches dreaming,
While enraptured sob the waterfalls,
Great fountains suave against the marble gleaming.
                                                        P.T.

The Faun

An old terra cotta faun,
Centered on a measured lawn,
Laughs, implying fate to mean
That we will pay for those serene

Moments that have led us on
Until, sad pilgrims, we have seen

Jusqu'à cette heure dont la fuite
Tournoie au son des tambourins.

Fêtes galantes

Colloque sentimental

Dans le vieux parc solitaire et glacé
Deux formes ont tout à l'heure passé.

Leurs yeux sont morts et leurs lèvres sont molles,
Et l'on entend à peine leurs paroles.

Dans le vieux parc solitaire et glacé
Deux spectres ont évoqué le passé.

—Te souvient-il de notre extase ancienne?
—Pourquoi voulez-vous donc qu'il m'en souvienne?

—Ton cœur bat-il toujours à mon seul nom?
Toujours vois-tu mon âme en rêve?—Non.

—Ah! les beaux jours de bonheur indicible
Où nous joignions nos bouches!—C'est possible.

—Qu'il était bleu, le ciel, et grand, l'espoir!
—L'espoir a fui, vaincu, vers le ciel noir.

Tels ils marchaient dans les avoines folles,
Et la nuit seule entendit leurs paroles.

Fêtes galantes

This fleeting hour already gone,
Whirled away by a tambourine.

                                    P.T.

Sentimental Colloquy

In the frozen, desolate, old park,
Two forms were slowly walking through the dark.

Their eyes are dead, and their lips are weak;
Almost imperceptibly they speak.

In the park, now desolate and cold,
Two ghosts remembering the days of old.

"Can you forget the happiness we knew?"
"What good do you think remembering would do?"

"Your heart stirs to my name as long ago?
My soul is to your dreams familiar?" "No."

"Ah! Our love was boundless ecstasy,
When our mouths joined together!" "That may be."

"The blue above us, as our hopes were high!"
"Defeated hope has fled toward a black sky."

So they walked among the wind-blown grass,
With only night to hear them as they passed.

                                    P.T.

Spleen

Les roses étaient toutes rouges,
Et les lierres étaient tout noirs.

Chère, pour peu que tu te bouges,
Renaissent tous mes désespoirs.

Le ciel était trop bleu, trop tendre,
La mer trop verte et l'air trop doux.

Je crains toujours,—ce qu'est d'attendre!—
Quelque fuite atroce de vous.

Du houx à la feuille vernie
Et du luisant buis je suis las,

Et de la campagne infinie
Et de tout, fors de vous, hélas!

Aquarelles

Spleen

The roses were perfectly red,
And the ivy perfectly black.

Dearest, if you but turn your head,
My despairs come swiftly back.

Too tender was the sky, too blue,
Too green the sea, too soft the air.

Always I fear—what waiting can do!—
The pain if you should not be there.

I'm tired of gleaming holly,
And boxwood like lustrous glass,

And the land stretching out before me,
And everything but you, alas!

                                    P.T.

> Le rossignol, qui du haut d'une
> branche se regarde dedans, croit
> être tombé dans la rivière. Il est
> au sommet d'un chêne et toutefois
> il a peur de se noyer.
>
> (Cyrano de Bergerac)

L'ombre des arbres dans la rivière embrumée
    Meurt comme de la fumée,
Tandis qu'en l'air, parmi les ramures réelles,
    Se plaignent les tourterelles.

Combien, ô voyageur, ce paysage blême
    Te mira blême toi-même,
Et que tristes pleuraient, dans les hautes feuillées,
    Tes espérances noyées!

Mai, Juin 1892
               Ariettes oubliées

> The nightingale, looking down
> from a high branch, thinks it has
> fallen into the river. On top of an
> oak, it is still afraid of drowning.
>
> (Cyrano de Bergerac)

On the mistbound river the trees' shadow
    Floats away like smoke,
While in the air, among tangible leaves,
    The turtledove grieves.

O wanderer, this pallid scene was a view
    Of your pallor too!
How bitter was the weeping, high above ground,
    Of your hopes that drowned!

May, June 1892

                                 P.T.

Lautréamont ✠✠✠ 1846-70

Lautréamont's epic prose poem, *Les Chants de Maldoror* is an act of absolute defiance. It transforms traditional poetics through an ironic use of rhetorical figures and breaks with the great classical definitions first proposed by the poet Malherbe in the latter part of the sixteenth-century; it systematically rejects the sentimental approach that had marked so much of the production of Romantic poetry in his own century; and in particular, the self-gratifying sufferings of Alfred de Musset and the lachrymose gravity of Lamartine, exemplified in his poem, *Le Lac*.

But Lautréamont was also profoundly concerned with the redefinition of the rules of poetry in a post-classical period. He elaborated a new poetry which, as it degraded Renaissance mythological subjects and traditional rules of poetic structure, suggested alternatives that were equally, though oppositely, monumental in their scope and in their impact upon the reader. A materialist poet, one who took himself seriously (though at times with tongue in cheek), Lautréamont insisted that what he wrote was charged with venom and thus constituted a real threat to the reader. The message he proposed is well illustrated in the multiple meaning of the famous apostrophe: Hail to you, old ocean! which punctuates the end of many of the stanzas in the First Song. The salutation is a mocking variation on the Christian greeting to the Virgin for whom the poet substitutes the material grandeur of the ocean, defining it by the adjective old which carries both a negative and a positive connotation. In this manner, part of the complexity of the poet's statement is formed by the convergence of historical, literary, lexical, psychological as well as stylistic effects: all together, they combine to form a cohesive, self-contained series of nucleus pronouncements.

S.G.

Les Chants de Maldoror

Chant premier

. . . Je me propose, sans être ému, de déclamer à grande voix la strophe sérieuse et froide que vous allez entendre. Vous, faites attention à ce qu'elle contient, et gardez-vous de l'impression pénible qu'elle ne manquera pas de laisser, comme une flétrissure, dans vos imaginations troublées. Ne croyez pas que je sois sur le point de mourir, car je ne suis pas encore un squelette, et la vieillesse n'est pas collée à mon front. Ecartons en conséquence toute idée de comparaison avec le cygne, au moment où son existence s'envole, et ne voyez devant vous qu'un monstre, dont je suis heureux que vous ne puissiez pas apercevoir la figure; mais, moins horrible est-elle que son âme. Cependant, je ne suis pas un criminel . . . Assez sur ce sujet. Il n'y a pas longtemps que j'ai revu la mer et foulé le pont des vaisseaux, et mes souvenirs sont vivaces comme si je l'avais quittée la veille. Soyez néanmoins, si vous le pouvez, aussi calmes que moi, dans cette lecture que je me repens déjà de vous offrir, et ne rougissez pas à la pensée de ce qu'est le cœur humain. O poulpe, au regard de soie! toi, dont l'âme est inséparable de la mienne; toi, le plus beau des habitants du globe terrestre, et qui commandes à un sérail de quatre cents ventouses; toi, en qui siègent noblement, comme dans leur résidence naturelle, par un commun accord, d'un lien indestructible, la douce vertu communicative et les grâces divines, pourquoi n'es-tu pas avec moi, ton ventre de mercure contre ma poitrine d'aluminium, assis tous les deux sur quelque rocher du rivage, pour contempler ce spectacle que j'adore!

The Songs of Maldoror

First song

. . . I plan to declaim, in a powerful voice, and without emotions, this sober and serious stanza you are about to hear. Listen to what it contains and be forwarned about the painful impression it will undoubtedly make on you, like a branding iron on your troubled imaginations. Don't think that I am about to die, since I have not yet become a skeleton, and old age hasn't stuck itself to my forehead. Thus, let us dispense with all comparisons with the swan, at the moment when his life flies off; what you have before you is simply a monster whose face, I'm glad to say, you can't make out, but it is less horrible than his soul. Still, I am not a criminal . . . Enough on this subject. Not long ago, I saw the sea again and paced on ships' bridges, and my memories of it are as sharp as if I had been there yesterday. Nevertheless, if you can, try to be as calm as I am, as you read what I already regret offering you, and do not blush when you think about the meaning of man's heart. O octopus, with your silken gaze! you whose soul is inseparable from mine: you, the most beautiful creature of the terrestial globe, and who commands a harem of four hundred leeches; you, in whom one can find, and nobly, as in their natural habitat, and by common consent, in an indestructible bond, sweet communicative virtue and the divine graces, why aren't you with me, your mercury belly against my aluminum chest, both of us sitting on some rock on the shore, contemplating this view that I adore!

Vieil océan, aux vagues de cristal, tu ressembles proportionnellement à ces marques azurées que l'on voit sur le dos meurtri des mousses; tu es un immense bleu, appliqué sur le corps de la terre: j'aime cette comparaison. Ainsi, à ton premier aspect, un souffle prolongé de tristesse, qu'on croirait être le murmure de ta brise suave, passe, en laissant des ineffaçables traces sur l'âme profondément ébranlée, et tu rappelles au souvenir de tes amants, sans qu'on s'en rende toujours compte, les rudes commencements de l'homme, où il fait connaissance avec la douleur, qui ne le quitte plus. Je te salue, vieil océan!

Vieil océan, ta forme harmonieusement sphérique, qui réjouit la face grave de la géométrie, ne me rappelle que trop les petits yeux de l'homme, pareils à ceux du sanglier pour la petitesse, et à ceux des oiseaux de nuit pour la perfection circulaire du contour. Cependant, l'homme s'est cru beau dans tous les siècles. Moi, je suppose plutôt que l'homme ne croit à sa beauté que par amour-propre; mais, qu'il n'est pas beau réellement et qu'il s'en doute; car, pourquoi regarde-t-il la figure de son semblable avec tant de mépris? Je te salue, vieil océan!

Vieil océan, tu es le symbole de l'identité: toujours égal à toi-même. Tu ne varies pas d'une manière essentielle, et, si tes vagues sont quelque part en furie, plus loin, dans quelque autre zone, elles sont dans le calme le plus complet. Tu n'es pas comme l'homme, qui s'arrête dans la rue, pour voir deux bouledogues s'empoigner au cou, mais, qui ne s'arrête pas, quand un enterrement passe; qui est ce matin accessible et ce soir de mauvaise humeur; qui rit aujourd'hui et pleure demain. Je te salue, vieil océan!

Vieil océan, il n'y aurait rien d'impossible à ce que tu caches dans ton sein de futures utilités pour l'homme. Tu lui as déjà donné la baleine. Tu ne laisses pas facilement deviner aux yeux avides des sciences naturelles les mille secrets de ton in-

Old ocean, with crystal waves, you resemble, to an extent, those azure marks that one can see on the flayed backs of cabin-boys; you are an immense blue bruise on the earth's body: I like that comparison. Thus, upon your first appearance, an extended sigh of sadness passes, that might be mistaken for the murmur of your soft breeze which leaves indelible traces on a soul profoundly disturbed, and you remind your lovers, though they are not always conscious of it, of the difficult beginnings of man, when he was first acquainted with that pain which no longer leaves him. Hail to you, old ocean!

Old ocean, your harmoniously spherical shape that rejoices the somber face of geometry, reminds me only too vividly of man's small eyes, similar to the boar's in smallness, and to those of nightbirds for the perfection of their circular contours. Despite this, man has considered himself beautiful throughout the centuries. I rather think that man believes he is beautiful only out of vanity; but that, in truth, he is not beautiful, and he suspects it; otherwise, why would he look upon the face of his fellowmen with so much contempt? Hail to you, old ocean!

Old ocean, you are the symbol of identity: always even with yourself. You do not change in any essential way, and if somewhere your waves are in a state of fury, farther off, in some other zone, they are in the most complete state of calm. You are not like the man who stops in the street to watch two bulldogs go at each other's throats, but fails to stop when a funeral procession passes by; who is pleasant in the morning and gruff at night; who laughs today and weeps tomorrow. Hail to you, old ocean!

Old ocean, it would not be surprising if you concealed in your bosom future useful things for man. You have already given him the whale. You do not easily reveal to the avid gaze of the natural sciences the thousand secrets of your inmost or-

time organisation: tu es modeste. L'homme se vante sans cesse, et pour des minuties. Je te salue, vieil océan!

Vieil océan, les différentes espèces de poissons que tu nourris n'ont pas juré fraternité entre elles. Chaque espèce vit de son côté. Les tempéraments et les conformations qui varient dans chacune d'elles, expliquent, d'une manière satisfaisante, ce qui ne paraît d'abord qu'une anomalie. Il en est ainsi de l'homme, qui n'a pas les mêmes motifs d'excuse. Un morceau de terre est-il occupé par trente millions d'êtres humains, ceux-ci se croient obligés de ne pas se mêler de l'existence de leurs voisins, fixés comme des racines sur le morceau de terre qui suit. En descendant du grand au petit, chaque homme vit comme un sauvage dans sa tanière, et en sort rarement pour visiter son semblable, accroupi pareillement dans une autre tanière. La grande famille universelle des humains est une utopie digne de la logique la plus médiocre. En outre, du spectacle de tes mamelles fécondes, se dégage la notion d'ingratitude; car, on pense aussitôt à ces parents nombreux, assez ingrats envers le Créateur, pour abandonner le fruit de leur misérable union. Je te salue, vieil océan!

Vieil océan, ta grandeur matérielle ne peut se comparer qu'à la mesure qu'on se fait de ce qu'il a fallu de puissance active pour engendrer la totalité de ta masse. On ne peut pas t'embrasser d'un coup d'oeil. Pour te contempler, il faut que la vue tourne son télescope, par un mouvement continu, vers les quatre points de l'horizon, de même qu'un mathématicien, afin de résoudre une équation algébrique, est obligé d'examiner séparément les divers cas possibles, avant de trancher la difficulté. L'homme mange des substances nourrissantes, et fait d'autres efforts, dignes d'un meilleur sort, pour paraître gras. Qu'elle se gonfle tant qu'elle voudra, cette adorable grenouille. Sois tranquille, elle ne t'égalera pas en grosseur; je le suppose, du moins. Je te salue, vieil océan!

Vieil océan, tes eaux sont amères. C'est exactement le

ganization; you are modest. Man brags all the time, and for the merest details. Hail to you, old ocean!

Old ocean, the different species of fish that you nourish have not pledged fraternity among themselves. Each species lives by itself. The temperaments and the conformations that vary within each one explain, in a satisfying manner, what, at first glance, seems to be an anomaly. So is it with man but he hasn't the same excuses. If a piece of land is occupied by thirty million human beings, they feel obliged not to bother about the lives of their neighbors, fixed like roots in the adjoining piece of land. Going from the national to the individual, each man lives like a savage in his lair and rarely leaves it to visit his fellow man, similarly crouching in another lair. The great universal family of man is a utopia, worthy of the most mediocre logic. Furthermore, looking at your lifegiving breasts, one can derive the notion of ingratitude; for one immediately thinks about those numerous parents, sufficiently ungrateful to the Creator to abandon the fruit of their miserable union. Hail to you, old ocean!

Old ocean, your material grandeur can be judged only if one can imagine the vibrant power required to engender the totality of your mass. The eye cannot encompass you at a glance. In order to contemplate you, one's gaze must turn its telescope, in a continual movement, toward the four points of the horizon, in the same way that a mathematician, in order to solve an algebraic problem, is forced to examine separately the various possible solutions before resolving the difficulty. Man eats nourishing foods, and makes other efforts, worthy of a finer fate, in order to look as if he had put on weight. Let the adorable frog blow itself up as much as it wants to. Have no fear: it will never equal you in volume; at least, that's what I believe. Hail to you, old ocean!

Old ocean, your waters are bitter. They taste exactly like the bile that critics spew forth on the fine arts, on sciences, on

même goût que le fiel que distille la critique sur les beaux-arts, sur les sciences, sur tout. Si quelqu'un a du génie, on le fait passer pour un idiot; si quelque autre est beau de corps, c'est un bossu affreux. Certes, il faut que l'homme sente avec force son imperfection, dont les trois quarts d'ailleurs ne sont dus qu'à lui-même, pour la critiquer ainsi! Je te salue, vieil océan!

Vieil océan, les hommes, malgré l'excellence de leurs méthodes, ne sont pas encore parvenus, aidés par les moyens d'investigation de la science, à mesurer la profondeur vertigineuse de tes abîmes; tu en as que les sondes les plus longues, les plus pesantes, ont reconnu inaccessibles. Aux poissons . . . ça leur est permis: pas aux hommes. Souvent, je me suis demandé quelle chose était le plus facile à reconnaître: la profondeur de l'océan ou la profondeur du cœur humain! Souvent, la main portée au front, debout sur les vaisseaux, tandis que la lune se balançait entre les mâts d'une façon irrégulière, je me suis surpris, faisant abstraction de tout ce qui n'était pas le but que je poursuivais, m'efforçant de résoudre ce difficile problème! Oui, quel est le plus profond, le plus impénétrable des deux: l'océan ou le cœur humain? Si trente ans d'expérience de la vie peuvent jusqu'à un certain point pencher la balance vers l'une ou l'autre de ces solutions, il me sera permis de dire que, malgré la profondeur de l'océan, il ne peut pas se mettre en ligne, quant à la comparaison sur cette propriété, avec la profondeur du cœur humain. J'ai été en relation avec des hommes qui ont été vertueux. Ils mouraient à soixante ans, et chacun ne manquait pas de s'écrier: "Ils ont fait le bien sur cette terre, c'est-à-dire qu'ils ont pratiqué la charité: voilà tout, ce n'est pas malin, chacun peut en faire autant." Qui comprendra pourquoi deux amants qui s'idolâtraient la veille, pour un mot mal interprété, s'écartent, l'un vers l'orient, l'autre vers l'occident, avec les aiguillons de la haine, de la vengeance, de l'amour et du remords, et ne se revoient plus, chacun drapé dans sa fierté solitaire. C'est un

everything. If someone has genius, he is considered an idiot; if someone else has a handsome body, he's a hideous hunchback. No doubt, if he so criticizes his own imperfections, man must have felt them forcefully, besides, three quarters of them are of his own making! Hail to you, old ocean!

Old ocean, despite the excellence of their methods, men, aided by scientific means of investigation, have yet to measure the vertiginous depths of your abysses; there are some that the longest and the heaviest sounding lines have given up as unreachable. Fish are able to do it . . . men are not. I have often wondered what was easier to measure: the depth of the ocean or the depth of the human heart! Often, my hand raised to my forehead, standing on board ship, while the moon balanced itself precariously among the masts, I would forget everything that was not pertinent to the question that I was then interested in, and catch myself trying to resolve this difficult problem! Yes, which one is the deeper, the more impenetrable of the two: the ocean or the human heart? If thirty years of life's experience, can, up to a point, weigh the scale toward the one or the other of these solutions, may I be permitted to say that, despite the depth of the ocean, it cannot begin to compare, insofar as that quality is concerned, with the depth of the human heart. I have had dealings with men who acted virtuously. They would die at sixty, and no one ever failed to cry out: "They have helped others on this earth, that is to say, they have been charitable: that's all, that's not so clever. Anybody can do the same." Is it possible that two lovers who, the night before, idolized each other, can, over a word that has been misinterpreted, leave each other and never see each other again, one going toward the east and the other toward the west, goaded by hate, vengeance, love, and remorse, each one clothed in his solitary pride? This is a miracle that occurs every day and yet is still miraculous. How is it possible we enjoy the general misfortunes of our fellowmen, and

miracle qui se renouvelle chaque jour et qui n'en est pas moins miraculeux. Qui comprendra pourquoi l'on savoure non seulement les disgrâces générales de ses semblables, mais encore les particulières de ses amis les plus chers, tandis que l'on est affligé en même temps? Un exemple incontestable pour clore la série: l'homme dit hypocritement oui et pense non. C'est pour cela que les marcassins de l'humanité ont tant de confiance les uns dans les autres et ne sont pas égoïstes. Il reste à la psychologie beaucoup de progrès à faire. Je te salue, vieil océan!

Vieil océan, tu es si puissant, que les hommes l'ont appris à leurs propres dépens. Ils ont beau employer toutes les ressources de leur génie . . . incapables de te dominer. Ils ont trouvé leur maître. Je dis qu'ils ont trouvé quelque chose de plus fort qu'eux. Ce quelque chose a un nom. Ce nom est: l'océan! La peur que tu leur inspires est telle, qu'ils te respectent. Malgré cela, tu fais valser leurs plus lourdes machines avec grâce, élégance et facilité. Tu leur fais faire des sauts gymnastiques jusqu'au ciel, et des plongeons admirables jusqu'au fond de tes domaines: un saltimbanque en serait jaloux. Bienheureux sont-ils, quand tu ne les enveloppes pas définitivement dans tes plis bouillonnants, pour aller voir, sans chemin de fer, dans tes entrailles aquatiques, comment se portent les poissons, et surtout comment ils se portent eux-mêmes. L'homme dit: "Je suis plus intelligent que l'océan." C'est possible; c'est même assez vrai; mais l'océan lui est plus redoutable que lui à l'océan: c'est ce qu'il n'est pas nécessaire de prouver. Ce patriarche observateur, contemporain des premières époques de notre globe suspendu, sourit de pitié, quand il assiste aux combats navals des nations. Voilà une centaine de léviathans qui sont sortis des mains de l'humanité. Les ordres emphatiques supérieurs, les cris des blessés, les coups de canon, c'est du bruit fait exprès pour anéantir quelques secondes. Il paraît que le drame est fini, et que l'océan a

even the particular ones of our friends, even as we suffer over them? Here, to conclude this series, is an example no one can argue with: man says hypocritically Yes and thinks No. That is the reason the young wild boars of humanity have so much confidence in each other and are not egoists. Psychology still has a long road to travel. Hail to you, old ocean!

Old ocean, you are so powerful; men have learned that at their own expense. Though they call upon all the resources at their command . . . still they cannot rule over you. They have found their master. I say that they have found something stronger than themselves. This something has a name. That name is: the ocean! The fear you inspire in them is such that they respect you. Despite that, you make their heaviest machines waltz with grace, elegance, and ease. You make them perform gymnastic leaps that reach the clouds, and glorious dives that reach the depth of your domains: a tumbler would be jealous. How fortunate they are, when you do not envelop them definitively in your boiling folds, to go and see, without a railroad, inside your aquatic entrails, how the fish are feeling, and especially, how they feel themselves. Man says: "I am more intelligent than the ocean." That's possible; probably true, but he fears the ocean more than the ocean fears him. There is no need to demonstrate that. This observant patriarch, contemporary of the first epochs of our suspended globe, smiles out of pity, when he watches navies engage in combat. There go a hundred leviathans fashioned by the hands of humanity. The emphatic orders of the superior officers, the cries of the wounded, the cannon blasts, those are noises expressly made to destroy a few seconds. It seems the drama is over, and the ocean has placed everything in its belly. Its maw is formidable. It must be vast towards the bottom, in the direction of the unknown! Finally, to crown this rather dull and witless comedy, one can see a stork in the clouds, slowed by fatigue, screeching, without its wingspan faltering: "My, my

tout mis dans son ventre. La gueule est formidable. Elle doit être grande vers le bas, dans la direction de l'inconnu! Pour couronner enfin la stupide comédie, qui n'est pas même intéressante, on voit, au milieu des airs, quelque cigogne, attardée, par la fatigue, qui se met à crier, sans arrêter l'envergure de son vol: "Tiens! . . . je la trouve mauvaise! Il y avait en bas des points noirs; j'ai fermé les yeux: ils ont disparu." Je te salue, vieil océan!

Vieil océan, ô grand célibataire, quand tu parcours la solitude solennelle de tes royaumes flegmatiques, tu t'enorgueillis à juste titre de ta magnificence native, et des éloges vrais que je m'empresse de te donner. Balancé voluptueusement par les mols effluves de ta lenteur majestueuse, qui est le plus grandiose parmi les attributs dont le souverain pouvoir t'a gratifié, tu déroules, au milieu d'un sombre mystère, sur toute ta surface sublime, tes vagues incomparables, avec le sentiment calme de ta puissance éternelle. Elles se suivent parallèlement, séparées par de courts intervalles. A peine l'une diminue, qu'une autre va à sa rencontre en grandissant, accompagnée du bruit mélancolique de l'écume qui se fond, pour nous avertir que tout est écume. (Ainsi, les êtres humains, ces vagues vivantes, meurent l'un après l'autre, d'une manière monotone; mais, sans laisser de bruit écumeux.) L'oiseau de passage se repose sur elles avec confiance, et se laisse abandonner à leurs mouvements, pleins d'une grâce fière, jusqu'à ce que les os de ses ailes aient recouvré leur vigueur accoutumée pour continuer le pèlerinage aérien. Je voudrais que la majesté humaine ne fût que l'incarnation du reflet de la tienne. Je demande beaucoup, et ce souhait sincère est glorieux pour toi. Ta grandeur morale, image de l'infini, est immense comme la réflexion du philosophe, comme l'amour de la femme, comme la beauté divine de l'oiseau, comme les méditations de poète. Te es plus beau que la nuit. Réponds-moi, océan, veux-tu être mon frère? Remue-toi avec im-

. . . that sure was a nasty trick! There were some black spots down below; I closed my eyes: they've disappeared." Hail to you, old ocean!

Old ocean, great celibate, as you cover the solemn solitudes of your flegmatic kingdoms, there are good reasons why you should be proud of your innate magnificence, and of the true praises that I hasten to offer to you. Voluptuously swayed by the soft effluvia of your majestic slowness, which is the most grandiose of all those attributes the sovereign power bestowed upon you, you unfurl your peerless waves, in the midst of a dark mystery, over all your sublime surface, sure of the knowledge of your eternal strength. They follow in parallels, separated by short intervals. One has hardly fallen, then another rises to meet it, accompanied by the melancholy sound of liquefying foam to warn us that everything is foam. (In this fashion, men, those living waves, die, one after the other, in a monotonous manner; but without leaving behind them the sound of foam.) The migratory bird rests on them with confidence, and yielding itself to their movements, full of a proud grace, until the bones of its wings have recovered their customary vigor and then it continues on its aerial pilgrimage. I would wish that human majesty might be the incarnate reflection of your own. I am asking a lot, and this sincere wish adds to your glory. Your moral grandeur, image of the infinite, is as boundless as the philosopher's reflection, as a woman's love, as the divine beauty of a bird, as the poet's meditations. You are more beautiful than the night. Answer me, ocean, do you want to be my brother? Rouse yourself impetuously . . . more . . . still more, if you want me to compare you to God's vengeance; extend your livid claws, as you make a path for yourself on your own breast . . . good. Unfurl your dreadful waves, hideous ocean, that I alone can understand, and in front of whom I fall, prostrate at your knees. Man's majesty is borrowed: he does not impress me: you do.

pétuosité . . . plus . . . plus encore, si tu veux que je te
compare à la vengeance de Dieu; allonge tes griffes livides, en
te frayant un chemin sur ton propre sein . . . c'est bien.
Déroule tes vagues épouvantables, océan hideux, compris par
moi seul, et devant lequel je tombe, prosterné à tes genoux.
La majesté de l'homme est empruntée; il ne m'imposera point:
toi, oui. Oh! quand tu t'avances, la crête haute et terrible,
entouré de tes replis tortueux comme d'une cour, magnétiseur
et farouche, roulant tes ondes les unes sur les autres, avec
la conscience de ce que tu es, pendant que tu pousses, des
profondeurs de ta poitrine, comme accablé d'un remords
intense que je ne puis pas découvrir, ce sourd mugissement
perpétuel que les hommes redoutent tant, même quand
ils te contemplent, en sûreté, tremblants sur le rivage, alors,
je vois qu'il ne m'appartient pas, le droit insigne de me dire
ton égal. C'est pourquoi, en présence de ta supériorité, je
te donnerais tout mon amour (et nul ne sait la quantité
d'amour que contiennent mes aspirations vers le beau), si tu
ne me faisais douloureusement penser à mes semblables, qui
forment avec toi le plus ironique contraste, l'antithèse la plus
bouffonne que l'on ait jamais vue dans la création: je ne puis
pas t'aimer, je te déteste. Pourquoi reviens-je à toi, pour la
millième fois, vers tes bras amis, qui s'entr'ouvrent, pour
caresser mon front brûlant, qui voit disparaître la fièvre à leur
contact! Je ne connais pas ta destinée cachée; tout ce qui te
concerne m'intéresse. Dis-moi donc si tu es la demeure du
prince des ténèbres. Dis-le-moi . . . dis-le-moi, océan (à moi
seul, pour ne pas attrister ceux qui n'ont encore connu que les
illusions), et si le souffle de Satan crée les tempêtes qui soulè-
vent tes eaux salées jusqu'aux nuages. Il faut que tu me le
dises, parce que je me réjouirais de savoir l'enfer si près de
l'homme. Je veux que celle-ci soit la dernière strophe de mon
invocation. Par conséquent, une seule fois encore, je veux **te**
saluer et te faire mes adieux! Vieil océan, aux vagues de cris-

Oh! when you come forward, your crest high and awesome, surrounded by your tortuous folds, like a court, mesmeric and fierce, rolling your waves one over the other, conscious of who you are, as you thrust upward, from the depths of your bosom, as if overwhelmed by an intense remorse that I am unable to discover, this perpetual muted roar that men are afraid of even when they contemplate you in safety, trembling on the shore. Then I understand it is not for me to rival with you. That is why, in the presence of your superiority, I would give all my love (and no one knows how much love there is in my aspirations toward beauty), if only you didn't make me sadly think of those who are like me, who form with you the most ironic contrast, the most clownlike antithesis that has ever been seen in all of creation: I cannot love you, I loathe you. Why do I come back to you, for the thousandth time, to your friendly arms that open and caress my burning forehead, that sees the fever disappear at their touch! I do not know your secret destiny; everything which concerns you interests me. Tell me, therefore, if you are the abode of the Prince of Darkness. Tell me . . . tell me, ocean (to me alone, so as not to sadden those who up to now know only illusions), and if Satan's breath creates the storms that heave your salty waters to the clouds. You must tell me, because I would rejoice to know that Hell is so close to man. I want this to be the last stanza of my invocation. Consequently, for the last time, I want to hail you and bid you farewell! Old ocean, with crystal waves . . . My eyes are filled with flowing tears, and I cannot go on; for I feel the time has come to return among men, with their brutish appearance; but . . . take heart! Let us make one last effort, and let us fulfill, with a sense of duty, our destiny upon this earth. Hail to you, old ocean!

S.G.

tal . . . Mes yeux se mouillent de larmes abondantes, et je n'ai pas la force de poursuivre; car, je sens que le moment est venu de revenir parmi les hommes, à l'aspect brutal; mais . . . courage! Faisons un grand effort, et accomplissons, avec le sentiment du devoir, notre destinée sur cette terre. Je te salue, vieil océan!

Arthur Rimbaud ✠✠✠ 1854–91

Rimbaud believed that what is required of a poet is superior vision, in every sense of the word—that he must be a *voyant*, a seer, who functions as a source of unique knowledge. We do not know whether he thought that in writing *Les Illuminations*, his last work, he had satisfied this definition. Did he stop writing poetry at the age of twenty-five because he had lost his convictions, or had he simply lost interest in them, preferring to explore Abyssinia rather than language?

While the most interesting of Rimbaud's early poems, traditionalistic in form and abrasively realistic in content, reflect his admiration for such predecessors as Hugo and Baudelaire, *Les Illuminations* has no significant antecedents. In this work Rimbaud expands the possibilities of language, infusing it with a new and more powerful energy. The poems seem not so much derived from experience, as experiences in themselves, which occur as the words pass into the mind of the reader. Interpretations ranging from the influence of hashish to that of sexual experimentation have seemed, however fascinating, beside the point. *Une Saison en enfer* may be more relevant when it speaks of the morose unity of the self exploding into a vehement multiplicity. That explosion, in turn, initiates Rimbaud's project: to liberate the world of objects from the empire of habit and reason. In "Fleurs," for example, a particular garden may well have been the occasion for the poem, but the "rose d'eau" has a reality independent of orthodox flowers, while the foxglove and the more conventional roses in its neighborhood derive their strength from something other than roots in the soil. The poem has the authority of an organic unity; it is not a logical argument, but a presence.

P.T.

Aube

J'ai embrassé l'aube d'été.

Rien ne bougeait encore au front des palais. L'eau était morte. Les camps d'ombres ne quittaient pas la route du bois. J'ai marché, réveillant les haleines vives et tièdes, et les pierreries regardèrent, et les ailes se levèrent sans bruit.

La première entreprise fut, dans le sentier déjà empli de frais et blêmes éclats, une fleur qui me dit son nom.

Je ris au wasserfall blond qui s'échevela à travers les sapins: à la cime argentée je reconnus la déesse.

Alors je levai un à un les voiles. Dans l'allée, en agitant les bras. Par la plaine, où je l'ai dénoncée au coq. A la grand'ville elle fuyait parmi les clochers et les dômes, et courant comme un mendiant sur les quais de marbre, je la chassais.

En haut de la route, près d'un bois de lauriers, je l'ai entourée avec ses voiles amassés, et j'ai senti un peu son immense corps. L'aube et l'enfant tombèrent au bas du bois.

Au réveil il était midi.

Illuminations

Dawn

I have embraced the summer dawn.

The palace façades were still impassive. The water was dead. The shadows remained encamped on the road through the woods. My footsteps awakened a warm and living breath; the gemstones watched, and silent wings arose.

The first enterprise: in a path already sparkling with cool and pallid light, a flower told me its name.

I laughed as the blond waterfall rushed dishevelled among the pines: by its silvery summit I recognized the goddess.

Then I drew aside the veils, one by one. Down the path, waving my arms. Through the plain where I betrayed her to the cock. She fled among the domes and steeples of the city, and running like a beggar along the marble wharfs, I pursued.

Far up the road, near a laurel wood, I surrounded her with the gathered veils, and I felt something of her immense body. Dawn and the child fell down to the depths of the woods.

When I awoke, it was noon.

P.T.

Les Ponts

Des ciels gris de cristal. Un bizarre dessin de ponts, ceux-ci droits, ceux-là bombés, d'autres descendant ou obliquant en angles sur les premiers, et ces figures se renouvelant dans les autres circuits éclairés du canal, mais tous tellement longs et légers que les rives, chargées de dômes, s'abaissent et s'amoindrissent. Quelques-uns de ces ponts sont encore chargés de masures. D'autres soutiennent des mâts, des signaux, de frêles parapets. Des accords mineurs se croisent et filent, des cordes montent des berges. On distingue une veste rouge, peut-être d'autres costumes et des instruments de musique. Sont-ce des airs populaires, des bouts de concerts seigneuriaux, des restants d'hymnes publics? L'eau est grise et bleue, large comme un bras de mer. —Un rayon blanc, tombant du haut du ciel, anéantit cette comédie.

Illuminations

Vagabonds

Pitoyable frère! Que d'atroces veillées je lui dus! "Je ne me saisissais pas fervemment de cette entreprise. Je m'étais joué de son infirmité. Par ma faute nous retournerions en exil, en esclavage." Il me supposait un guignon et une innocence très bizarres, et il ajoutait des raisons inquiétantes.

Bridges

Skies of crystal grey. A bizarre composition of bridges, flat ones here, arched ones over there, others coming down straight or obliquely across the first, and these patterns repeating themselves in the other lighted channels of the canal, but all the bridges so long and buoyant that the banks, heavy with domes, sink down and diminish. A few of these bridges are still burdened with huts. Others hold up masts, signals, fragile parapets. Minor chords cross and spin away, taut cords rise from the water's edge. You can make out a red jacket, other costumes perhaps, and musical instruments. Are those popular tunes, fragments of lordly recitals, shards of ceremonial hymns? The water is grey and blue, broad as an arm of the sea. —A ray of white light, falling all the way down from the sky, puts an end to the performance.

P.T.

Vagabonds

Pitiful brother! How many atrocious nights without sleep he gave me! "My commitment to the enterprise lacked fervor. I had made fun of his weakness. It was my fault that we'd be exiled, enslaved again." He assumed that I was jinxed, and just as bizarrely innocent, for which he offered worrisome explanations.

Je répondais en ricanant à ce satanique docteur, et finissais par gagner la fenêtre. Je créais, par delà la campagne traversée par des bandes de musique rare, les fantômes du futur luxe nocturne.

Après cette distraction vaguement hygiénique, je m'étendais sur une paillasse. Et, presque chaque nuit, aussitôt endormi, le pauvre frère se levait, la bouche pourrie, les yeux arrachés,—tel qu'il se rêvait!—et me tirait dans la salle en hurlant son songe de chagrin idiot.

J'avais en effet, en toute sincérité d'esprit, pris l'engagement de le rendre à son état primitif de fils du Soleil,—et nous errions, nourris du vin des cavernes et du biscuit de la route, moi pressé de trouver le lieu et la formule.

Illuminations

Vies

I

O les énormes avenues du pays saint, les terrasses du temple! Qu'a-t-on fait du brahmane qui m'expliqua les Proverbes? D'alors, de là-bas, je vois encore même les vieilles! Je me souviens des heures d'argent et de soleil vers les fleuves, la main de la campagne sur mon épaule, et de nos caresses debout dans les plaines poivrées.—Un envol de pigeons écarlates tonne autour de ma pensée.—Exilé ici, j'ai eu une scène où jouer les chefs-d'œuvre dramatiques de toutes les littératures. Je vous indiquerais les richesses inouïes. J'observe l'histoire des trésors que vous trouvâtes. Je vois la suite! Ma sagesse est aussi dédaignée que le chaos. Qu'est mon néant, auprès de la stupeur qui vous attend?

I would answer the diabolical doctor with a sneer, finally taking leave of him through the window. I created, on the other side of a landscape traversed by bands of exotic music, phantasms of the opulent nights to come.

After that vaguely hygienic distraction, I would stretch out on a straw mat. And, almost every night, as soon as I fell asleep, the poor brother would get up, mouth rotting, eyes torn out—just as he imagined himself!—and drag me into the room, howling his imbecilic dream of sorrow.

It's true that I had, in all sincerity, undertaken to restore him to his original condition, as child of the Sun—and so we wandered, living on cavern wine and hardtack, with me in a hurry to find the place and the formula.

P.T.

Lives

I

O the vast avenues of the holy land, the terraces of the temple! What happened to the Brahman who explained the Vedas to me? From that time and that place I can still see even the old women. I remember the hours of silver and of sunlight close to the rivers, the landscape's hand on my shoulder, and how we embraced as we stood in the aromatic plains.—A flight of scarlet pigeons thunders around my thought.—Here, in exile, I've had a stage fit for the whole world's masterpieces of drama. I'd like to tell you where incredible riches are. Before my eyes is the history of the treasures you once found. I see what follows! My wisdom will be scorned as chaos is. How can my nothingness compare to the stupor waiting for you?

II

Je suis un inventeur bien autrement méritant que tous ceux qui m'ont précédé; un musicien même, qui ai trouvé quelque chose comme la clef de l'amour. A présent, gentilhomme d'une campagne aigre au ciel sobre, j'essaye de m'émouvoir au souvenir de l'enfance mendiante, de l'apprentissage ou de l'arrivée en sabots, des polémiques, des cinq ou six veuvages, et quelques noces où ma forte tête m'empêcha de monter au diapason des camarades. Je ne regrette pas ma vieille part de gaîté divine: l'air sobre de cette aigre campagne alimente fort activement mon atroce scepticisme. Mais comme ce scepticisme ne peut désormais être mis en œuvre, et que d'ailleurs je suis dévoué à un trouble nouveau,—j'attends de devenir un très méchant fou.

III

Dans un grenier où je fus enfermé à douze ans j'ai connu le monde, j'ai illustré la comédie humaine. Dans un cellier j'ai appris l'histoire. A quelque fête de nuit dans une cité du Nord, j'ai rencontré toutes les femmes des anciens peintres. Dans un vieux passage à Paris on m'a enseigné les sciences classiques. Dans une magnifique demeure cernée par l'Orient entier j'ai accompli mon immense œuvre et passé mon illustre retraite. J'ai brassé mon sang. Mon devoir m'est remis. Il ne faut même plus songer à cela. Je suis réellement d'outre-tombe, et pas de commissions.

Illuminations

II

I'm an inventor far more deserving than my predecessors, a musician, in fact, having found what you might call the key of love. These days, lord of a bitter landscape, under a sober sky, I try to feel sentimental as I remember a mendicant childhood, apprenticeship or my grand entrance in wooden shoes, polemics, five or six bereavements, and a few celebrations when my hard head prevented my attaining the diapason of my companions. I don't miss sharing the laughter of the gods: the sober air of this bitter landscape all too effectively feeds my atrocious scepticism. But since there's nothing to be done with that scepticism now, and besides I am committed to a whole new disorder—I expect to become a very nasty madman.

III

I discovered the world in an attic where they shut me up when I was twelve; I illustrated the human comedy. I learned history in a cellar. On some gala night in a northern city, I met the women of all the old masters. I studied the classical sciences in an old Parisian passageway. Where all the orient encircled my princely residence, my immense work was completed, and I went into illustrious retirement. I have brewed my blood. My obligation is cancelled. Better not even to think of that again. I am really from beyond the grave, and nobody's errand boy.

P.T.

Fleurs

D'un gradin d'or,—parmi les cordons de soie, les gazes grises, les velours verts et les disques de cristal qui noircissent comme du bronze au soleil,—je vois la digitale s'ouvrir sur un tapis de filigranes d'argent, d'yeux et de chevelures.

Des pièces d'or jaune semées sur l'agate, des piliers d'acajou supportant un dôme d'émeraudes, des bouquets de satin blanc et de fines verges de rubis entourent la rose d'eau.

Tels qu'un dieu aux énormes yeux bleus et aux formes de neige, la mer et le ciel attirent aux terrasses de marbre la foule des jeunes et fortes roses.

Illuminations

Mystique

Sur la pente du talus les anges tournent leurs robes de laine dans les herbages d'acier et d'émeraude.

Des prés de flammes bondissent jusqu'au sommet du mamelon. À gauche le terreau de l'arête est piétiné par tous les homicides et toutes les batailles, et tous les bruits désastreux filent leur courbe. Derrière l'arête de droite la ligne des orients, des progrès.

Et tandis que la bande en haut du tableau est formée de la rumeur tournante et bondissante des conques des mers et des nuits humaines,

Flowers

From golden steps—among the silken ropes, the grey gauzes, green velvets, and the crystal disks that darken like bronze in the sun—I watch the foxglove opening its fingers on a carpet of filigreed silver, eyes, and tresses of hair.

Yellow-gold coins strewn over the agate, mahogany pillars supporting an emerald dome, white satin bouquets, and slender wands of rubies surround the water rose.

Like a god with enormous blue eyes and the contours of snow, the sea and the sky attract the crowd of strong, young roses to the terraces of marble.

P.T.

Mystic

On the slope of the hillside, angels are turning their robes of wool in the steel and emerald grasses.

Meadows of flame leap up to the crest of the knoll. To the left the ridge has been trampled by all the murders, all the battles, and all the disastrous noises spin out their curve. Behind the ridge, to the right, the line of the orients, of progress.

And while the band at the top of the picture is made of the revolving and bounding sounds of conch shells of the seas and human nights,

La douceur fleurie des étoiles et du ciel et du reste descend en face du talus, comme un panier,—contre notre face, et fait l'abîme fleurant et bleu là-dessous.

Illuminations

Being Beauteous

Devant une neige un Être de Beauté de haute taille. Des sifflements de mort et des cercles de musique sourde font monter, s'élargir et trembler comme un spectre ce corps adoré; des blessures écarlates et noires éclatent dans les chairs superbes. Les couleurs propres de la vie se foncent, dansent, et se dégagent autour de la Vision, sur le chantier. Et les frissons s'élèvent et grondent, et la saveur forcenée de ces effets se chargeant avec les sifflements mortels et les rauques musiques que le monde, loin derrière nous, lance sur notre mère de beauté,—elle recule, elle se dresse. Oh! nos os sont revêtus d'un nouveau corps amoureux.

O la face cendrée, l'écusson de crin, les bras de cristal! Le canon sur lequel je dois m'abattre à travers la mêlée des arbres et de l'air léger!

Illuminations

The flowery sweetness of the stars and the sky and all the rest comes down in front of the hillside like a basket— right before our eyes, and forms the blue and fragrant abyss below.

P.T.

Being Beauteous

In front of snow, a lofty Presence of Beauty. Whistlings of death and circles of muffled music make the beloved body rise, expand, and tremble like a spectre; black and scarlet wound explode in the magnificent flesh. The colors of life itself rush into the workyard, dance, and break away around the Vision. Vibrations of fear rise and growl, and when the frenzied taste of all this takes on the lethal hissing, the hoarse music that the world, far behind us, casts at our mother of beauty—she steps back, she straightens. Oh! our bones are clad in a new and loving body.

O the ashen face, the haircloth shield, the crystal arms! The cannon where I'll come to slaughter, across the joined battle of trees and the gentle air!

P.T.

Jules Laforgue ✠✠✠ 1860-87

When Laforgue developed his gift for irony, he found a way to convert the frustrations, mediocrities, and failures of his life into the values of art. To say "Ah! this Life is so everyday . . ." is simultaneously to defeat bordeom and dominate experience. One would even risk becoming a kind of existentialist hero, if the master of irony weren't automatically self-deflating. Perhaps the therapeutic effort of this technique accounts for the zest which prevails in the poems. No matter to what extent they disown the hopes and pretensions of life, they are in themselves a positive statement. When, for example, the poet imagines Her, writhing on the mat he had "just for that purpose" put in front of his door, he is like an anatomist whose dissection reveals the whole fine structure of self-delusion and mockery and the endless disappointments of the tête-à-tête, leaving it all intact, and, by virtue of being visible, a fit object for aesthetic contemplation. This was the skill T. S. Eliot acquired from Laforgue; it is responsible for Prufrock, although certainly not for the *Four Quartets*.

Laforgue put the absolutely relative Moon in the place of *l'Azur*, and Pierrot in place of himself. So disguised, he could turn away from the world, and call it his own.

P.T.

Autre Complainte de Lord Pierrot

Celle qui doit me mettre au courant de la Femme!
Nous lui dirons d'abord, de mon air le moins froid:
"La somme des angles d'un triangle, chère âme,
     "Est égale à deux droits."

Et si ce cri lui part: "Dieu de Dieu! que je t'aime!"
—"Dieu reconnaîtra les siens." Ou piquée au vif:
—"Mes claviers ont du cœur, tu seras mon seul thème."
     Moi: "Tout est relatif."

De tous ses yeux, alors! se sentant trop banale:
"Ah! tu ne m'aimes pas; tant d'autres sont jaloux!"
Et moi, d'un œil qui vers l'Inconscient s'emballe:
     "Merci, pas mal; et vous?"

—"Jouons au plus fidèle!"—"A quoi bon, ô Nature!"
"Autant à qui perd gagne!" Alors, autre couplet:
—"Ah! tu te lasseras le premier, j'en suis sûre . . ."
     —"Après vous, s'il vous plaît."

Enfin, si, par un soir, elle meurt dans mes livres,
Douce; feignant de n'en pas croire encor mes yeux,
J'aurai un: "Ah çà, mais, nous avions De Quoi vivre!
     "C'était donc sérieux?"

                                        Les Complaintes

Another Complaint of Lord Pierrot

She who is to put me in touch with Woman!
Let's say to her, with a benevolent stare,
"The sum of a triangle's angles, dear soul,
    Equals just two square."

And if she should cry out, "Oh God! I love you so!"
"God will look after His own." Or, pierced to the quick,
"You make my heartstrings sing! You're why I live!"
    I: "Everything's relative."

Then, with blazing eyes, renouncing banality:
"Oh, you don't love me—and there are others who do!"
And I, bolting away toward the Unconscious,
    "Thanks, not bad, and you?"

"Let's play Fidelity!" "O Nature, what's the use?"
"But winners lose!" And then, *reprise:*
"Ah! you'll get tired of me first, I'm sure . . ."
    "After you, if you please."

And at last if, sweetly, one evening, she dies in my books,
Unable to trust my eyes, I'll be invoking,
"How could you! When we had So Much to live for!
    I thought you were only joking."

                        P.T.

Complainte sur certains ennuis

Un couchant des Cosmogonies!
Ah! que la Vie est quotidienne . . .
Et, du plus vrai qu'on se souvienne,
Comme on fut piètre et sans génie . . .

On voudrait s'avouer des choses,
Dont on s'étonnerait en route,
Qui feraient, une fois pour toutes!
Qu'on s'entendrait à travers poses.

On voudrait saigner le Silence,
Secouer l'exil des causeries;
Et non! ces dames sont aigries
Par des questions de préséance.

Elles boudent là, l'air capable.
Et, sous les ciels, plus d'un s'explique,
Par quel gâchis suresthétiques
Ces êtres-là sont adorables.

Justement, une nous appelle,
Pour l'aider à chercher sa bague,
Perdue (où dans ce terrain vague?)
Un souvenir D'AMOUR, dit-elle!

Ces êtres-là sont adorables!
                              Les Complaintes

Complaint About Certain Annoyances

A sunset of Cosmogonies!
Ah! this Life is so everyday . . .
And, in the truth of memories,
Those paltry talents we display . . .

What of the things we wanted to tell,
To be astonishing *en route,*
Which were to make us, once and for all!
Understand each other beneath the shell.

We would like to bleed the Silence,
Shake off the exile of conversation;
But no! our ladies have grown sour,
Evaluating rank and station.

They pout now, alert but inactive.
And, under the sky, more than one of us wonders
By just what superaesthetic blunders
We find them so attractive.

Precisely! one of them summons me
To help look for her ring,
Lost (but where in this wilderness?)
"A souvenir of LOVE!" says she.

We find them *so* attractive.

                                             P.T.

Complainte de l'oubli des morts

Mesdames et Messieurs,
Vous dont la mère est morte,
C'est le bon fossoyeux
Qui gratte à votre porte.

Les morts
C'est sous terre;
Ça n'en sort
Guère.

Vous fumez dans vos bocks,
Vous soldez quelque idylle,
Là-bas chante le coq,
Pauvres morts hors des villes!

Grand-papa se penchait,
Là, le doigt sur la tempe,
Sœur faisait du crochet,
Mère montait la lampe.

Les morts
C'est discret,
Ça dort
Trop au frais.

Vous avez bien dîné,
Comment va cette affaire?
Ah! les petits mort-nés
Ne se dorlotent guère!

Complaint About Forgetting the Dead

Ladies and Gentlemen,
You whose mother is no more,
Listen! the good gravedigger's
Scratching at your door.

    The dead
  Underground
  Hardly ever
    Get around.

You blow in your beer,
Wrap up your dreams and pay;
There sings the chanticleer,
The poor dead, out of the way!

Grandfather would sway,
Heavy head on hand,
Sister did crochet,
Mother lit the lamp,

    The dead
  So discreet—
    Too much air
  Where they sleep.

You've enjoyed your dinner;
How was business today?
Ah! the stillborn babies
Haven't much chance to play.

Notez, d'un trait égal,
Au livre de la caisse,
Entre deux frais de bal:
Entretien tombe et messe.

    C'est gai,
  Cette vie;
  Hein, ma mie,
    O gué?

Mesdames et Messieurs,
Vous dont la sœur est morte,
Ouvrez au fossoyeux
Qui claque à votre porte;

Si vous n'avez pitié,
Il viendra (sans rancune)
Vous tirer par les pieds,
Une nuit de grand'lune!

    Importun
    Vent qui range!
    Les défunts?
    Ça voyage.
                 Les Complaintes

Tell that steady hand to place
Neatly in your budget,
Your wardrobe won't begrudge it,
Upkeep: mass and graves.

    Life's gay,
  Take a whirl,
  Eh! girl,
    O.K.?

Ladies and Gentlemen,
You whose sister is no more,
A welcome for the gravedigger
Banging on your door.

If you can't be polite,
He'll come (but not for spite)
And drag you by your feet
Into some moonlit night!

  Wild winds unravel
  Overhead!
  And the dead?
  Travel.

                 P.T.

Pierrots
(Scène courte, mais typique)

Il me faut, vos yeux! Dès que je perds leur étoile,
Le mal des calmes plats s'engouffre dans ma voile,
Le frisson du *Vae soli!* gargouille en mes moelles . . .

Vous auriez dû me voir après cette querelle!
J'errais dans l'agitation la plus cruelle,
Criant aux murs: Mon Dieu! mon Dieu! Que dira-t-elle?

Mais aussi, vrai, vous me blessâtes aux antennes
De l'âme, avec les mensonges de votre traîne.
Et votre tas de complications mondaines.

Je voyais que vos yeux me lançaient sur des pistes,
Je songeais: Oui, divins, ces yeux! mais rien n'existe
Derrière! Son âme est affaire d'oculiste.

Moi, je suis laminé d'esthétiques loyales!
Je hais les trémolos, les phrases nationales;
Bref, le violet gros deuil est ma couleur locale.

Je ne suis point "ce gaillard-là" ni Le Superbe!
Mais mon âme, qu'un cri un peu cru exacerbe,
Est au fond distinguée et franche comme une herbe.

J'ai des nerfs encor sensibles au son des cloches,
Et je vais en plein air sans peur et sans reproche,
Sans jamais me sourire en un miroir de poche.

Pierrots
(A short but typical scene)

But I need your eyes! As soon as I lose their rays
The sickness of dead calms engulfs my sails,
The shiver of *Vae soli!* [1] gurgles in my veins . . .

You should have seen me after that argument!
I wandered about in the cruelest torment,
Crying to the walls, "My God! My God! Will she relent?"

But just the same you wounded my soul's
Antennae with all your trailing lies
And all of those mundane complexities.

I saw your eyes were daring me to dare.
I thought, "Oh yes, divine! those eyes, but nothing's there
Behind them; her soul's an oculist's affair."

I'm made of aesthetics, laminated and true!
I hate the tremolo, the nationalistic hullabaloo;
In short, deep purple mourning's my native hue.

I'm neither "Quite the sport!" nor "He's superb!"
But my soul, which a cry that's raspy can disturb,
Is candid and distinguished, like an herb.

My nerves still respond to ringing bells I hear,
I go about in the open air, guileless and without fear,
And never, passing mirrors, stand and peer.

C'est vrai, j'ai bien roulé! J'ai râlé dans des gîtes
Peu vous; mais, n'en ai-je pas plus de mérite
A en avoir sauvé la foi en vos yeux? dites . . .

—Allons, faisons la paix. Venez, que je vous berce,
Enfant. Eh bien?
                            —C'est que, votre pardon me verse
Un mélange (confus) d'impressions . . . diverses . . .
                                                    (Exit)

                    L'Imitation de Notre-Dame la Lune

Oh! qu'une, d'Elle-même, un beau soir, sût venir
Ne voyant plus que boire à mes lèvres, ou mourir! . . .

Oh! Baptême!
Oh! baptême de ma Raison d'être!
Faire naître un "Je t'aime!"
Et qu'il vienne à travers les hommes et les dieux,
Sous ma fenêtre,
Baissant les yeux!

Qu'il vienne, comme à l'aimant la foudre,
Et dans mon ciel d'orage qui craque et qui s'ouvre,
Et alors, les averses lustrales jusqu'au matin,
Le grand clapissement des averses toute la nuit! Enfin
Qu'Elle vienne! et, baissant les yeux
Et s'essuyant les pieds
Au seuil de notre église, ô mes aïeux

It's true I've knocked around! I've spent myself in ways
Far from your own, but shouldn't keeping my faith
In your eyes merit, all the more, your praise?

"Oh, let's make up! Come and let me soothe you,
Child. What now?"
                            "But all this confession, you know,
And forgiveness . . . confuses me so . . ."

                                                    (*Exit*)

                                                    P.T.

[1] *Vae soli!* Latin: Alas, alone!

Oh! if one of Them, some fine evening would try—
Blind to all but drink at my lips, or die! . . .

Oh! Baptized!
Oh! my whole life's Reason baptized!
To give birth to an "I love you!"
That would travel across the Earth and skies,
And then under my window
Lower its eyes!

That would come like lightning toward magnets
Cracking open my stormy sky,
Then, until dawn, the lustral showers,
The great crying of showers all night long! At last
Let Her come! and lowering her eyes
And drying her feet
At the threshold of our church, O my ancestors,

Ministres de la Pitié,
Elle dise:

"Pour moi, tu n'es pas comme les autres hommes,
Ils sont ces messieurs, toi tu viens des cieux.
Ta bouche me fait baisser les yeux
Et ton port me transporte
Et je m'en découvre des trésors!
Et je sais parfaitement que ma destinée se borne
(Oh! j'y suis déjà bien habituée!)
À te suivre jusqu'à ce que tu te retournes,
Et alors t'exprimer comment tu es!

Vraiment je ne songe pas au reste; j'attendrai
Dans l'attendrissement de ma vie faite exprès.

Que je te dise seulement que depuis des nuits je pleure,
Et que mes sœurs ont bien peur que je n'en meure.

Je pleure dans les coins, je n'ai plus goût à rien;
Oh! j'ai tant pleuré dimanche dans mon paroissien!

Tu me demandes pourquoi toi et non un autre.
Ah! laisse, c'est bien toi et non un autre.

J'en suis sûre comme du vide insensé de mon cœur
Et comme de votre air mortellement moqueur."

Ainsi, elle viendrait, évadée, demi-morte,
Se rouler sur le paillasson que j'ai mis à cet effet devant ma
     porte.

Ainsi, elle viendrait à Moi avec des yeux absolument fous,
Et elle me suivrait avec ses yeux-là partout, partout!

Derniers Vers

Ministers of Compassion,
Let her repeat:

"You are so totally different from the others—
They're only men, but you, you come from Paradise.
Your mouth makes me lower my eyes,
And your gallant carriage carries me away,
And I find treasures all along the way!
And I know perfectly well my destiny is bound
(Oh, I'm quite accustomed to it already!)
To following you until you turn around,
And then to say how wonderful you are!

Truly, the rest means nothing to me; I'll wait
As tenderly as I exist for just this fate.

But let me tell you that all night long I cry,
And that my sisters are really afraid I'll die.

I sit in corners and weep; there's nothing I want to do.
My tears last Sunday drenched my prayerbook through!

You ask me why it's you and no one else.
Ah! believe me, it's you and no one else;

I know that as well as my heart's mad empty space,
Or the horribly mocking expression on your face."

Thus she would come, having fled, half-dead, to my door,
And writhe on the mat I had just for that purpose put there.

Thus she would come to Me with absolutely mad eyes,
And follow me with those eyes, everywhere, everywhere!
                                                    P.T.

Guillaume Apollinaire ✠✠✠ 1880-1918

Appollinaire, the illegitimate son of an Italian army officer and a Polish woman, maintained a double footing in his poetics that seemed to reflect his own origins. Always on the threshold of modernity, he perfected a theory of simultaneity whereby the poem, though sequentially written, sought to express the concurrent immediacy of reality. He introduced technical terms borrowed from an industrial and urban experience, contrary to post-symbolist aesthetics which favored a rather veiled and esoteric verbal atmosphere. He eliminated all punctuation, and most of all, he demystified poetry with a capital "P." As the letter-poem reveals, poetry no longer had to be the privileged expression of an ivory-tower poet. Apollinaire thought of himself as the spokesman for the new and, in 1917, coined the word surrealism to characterize *Parade,* a ballet to which Cocteau, Satie, and Picasso had contributed. But he was also a prudent and often uncertain individual who was equally attracted to classical order and to the past, to a nostalgic, melancholic, lyric disposition where the poet once again became the star-crossed lover, the solitary figure. In this guise, Apollinaire observed strict metrical requirements, used correct punctuation, and with few lexical divagations, adhered to the "noble" definition of poetry that had been fashioned by his nineteenth-century predecessors. This essential continuity-discontinuity with the past is best illustrated in the poem *The Pretty Redhead* where, after having tantalizingly sketched out the invisible marvels of a new world, he concludes in a despairing cry for pity, reminiscent of the most traditional voices of Christian poetry.

S.G.

La Jolie Rousse

Me voici devant tous un homme plein de sens
Connaissant la vie et de la mort ce qu'un vivant peut connaître
Ayant éprouvé les douleurs et les joies de l'amour
Ayant su quelquefois imposer ses idées
Connaissant plusieurs langages
Ayant pas mal voyagé
Ayant vu la guerre dans l'Artillerie et l'Infanterie
Blessé à la tête trépané sous le chloroforme
Ayant perdu ses meilleurs amis dans l'effroyable lutte
Je sais d'ancien et de nouveau autant qu'un homme seul
    pourrait des deux savoir
Et sans m'inquiéter aujourd'hui de cette guerre
Entre nous et pour nous mes amis
Je juge cette longue querelle de la tradition et de l'invention
    De l'Ordre de l'Aventure
Vous dont la bouche est faite à l'image de celle de Dieu
Bouche qui est l'ordre même
Soyez indulgents quand vous nous comparez
À ceux qui furent la perfection de l'ordre
Nous qui quêtons partout l'aventure

Nous ne sommes pas vos ennemis
Nous voulons vous donner de vastes et d'étranges domaines
Où le mystère en fleurs s'offre à qui veut le cueillir
Il y a là des feux nouveaux des couleurs jamais vues
Mille phantasmes impondérables
Auxquels il faut donner de la réalité

The Pretty Redhead

Here I stand in front of everybody a sensible man
Knowing life and about death what a living man can know
Having experienced the pains and the joys of love
Having at times been able to impose my views
Knowing several languages
Having traveled quite a bit
Having seen war in the Artillery and the Infantry
Wounded in the head trepanned under chloroform
Having lost his best friends in the fearful combat
I know about the old and the new as much as any one man
       could know about them both
And without being worried today about the war
Among ourselves and for us my friends
I weigh this long quarrel between tradition and invention
       Order and Adventure
You whose mouth is made in the image of God's
Mouth that is order itself
Be indulgent when you compare us
To those who were perfection of order
We who search out adventure everywhere

We are not your enemies
We want to give you vast and strange worlds
Where flowering mystery is there for anyone who wants to
       pick it
There there are new fires colors never seen
A thousand imponderable phantasms
That must be given reality

Nous voulons explorer la bonté contrée énorme où tout
    se tait
Il y a aussi le temps qu'on peut chasser ou faire revenir
Pitié pour nous qui combattons toujours aux frontières
De l'illimité et de l'avenir
Pitié pour nos erreurs pitié pour nos péchés
Voici que vient l'été la saison violente
Et ma jeunesse est morte ainsi que le printemps
O soleil c'est le temps de la Raison ardente
                Et j'attends
Pour la suivre toujours la forme noble et douce
Qu'elle prend afin que je l'aime seulement
Elle vient et m'attire ainsi qu'un fer l'aimant
           Elle a l'aspect charmant
           D'une adorable rousse
Ses cheveux sont d'or on dirait
Un bel éclair qui durerait
Ou ces flammes qui se pavanent
Dans les roses-thé qui se fanent
Mais riez riez de moi
Hommes de partout surtout gens d'ici
Car il y a tant de choses que je n'ose vous dire
Tant de choses que vous ne me laisseriez pas dire
Ayez pitié de moi

Calligrammes

4 h

C'est 4 h. du matin
Je me lève tout habillé

We want to explore kindness an enormous land where
    everything is still
There is also time that one can chase away or welcome back
Pity for us who are always fighting on the frontiers
Of the unlimited and the future
Pity for our errors pity for our sins
Here comes summer the violent season
And my youth is dead along with the springtime
O sun now is the time for fiery Reason
                    And I wait
To follow her for ever the sweet and noble shape
She takes for me to love it only
She comes and attracts me like iron the magnet
           She has the charming look
           Of an adorable redhead
Her hair is like gold one would say
A beautiful flash of lightning that would last
Or those flames promenading
Among tea roses fading
But laugh laugh at me
Men of everywhere especially men from around here
For there are so many things I dare not tell you
So many things you would not let me tell
Have pity on me

                                 S.G.

4 A.M.

It's four in the morning
I get up fully dressed

Je tiens une savonnette à la main
Que m'a envoyée quelqu'un que j'aime
Je vais me laver
Je sors du trou où nous dormons
Je suis dispos
Et content de pouvoir me laver ce qui n'est pas arrivé depuis
    trois jours
Puis lavé je vais me faire raser
Ensuite bleu de ciel je me confonds avec l'horizon jusqu'à la
    nuit et c'est un plaisir très doux
De ne rien dire de plus tout ce que je fais c'est un être
    invisible qui le fait
Puisqu'une fois boutonné tout bleu confondu dans le ciel je
    deviens invisible

Poèmes à Madeleine

Automne

Dans le brouillard s'en vont un paysan cagneux
Et son bœuf lentement dans le brouillard d'automne
Qui cache les hameaux pauvres et vergogneux

Et s'en allant là-bas le paysan chantonne
Une chanson d'amour et d'infidélité
Qui parle d'une bague et d'un cœur que l'on brise

Oh! l'automne l'automne a fait mourir l'été
Dans le brouillard s'en vont deux silhouettes grises

Alcools

I hold a piece of soap in my hand
Sent to me by someone I love
I'm going to wash
I get out of the trench where we sleep
I'm in good shape
And happy to wash I haven't done that in three days
Then washed I'll go and get shaved
Later in my sky-blue uniform I blend with the horizon until
      nightfall and it's a real pleasure
Not to add another word everything I do is done by an
      invisible being
Because once buttoned-up all blue I blend with the sky and
      become invisible

                                                      S.G.

Autumn

In the fog a knock-kneed peasant goes
Slowly with his ox in the autumn fog
That hides dirty little hamlets

And going in that direction the peasant hums
A song of love and infidelity
That speaks of a ring and a broken heart

Oh! autumn autumn has made the summer pass away
In the fog two gray silhouettes move on their way

                                                      S.G.

Nuit rhénane

Mon verre est plein d'un vin trembleur comme une flamme
Écoutez la chanson lente d'un batelier
Qui raconte avoir vu sous la lune sept femmes
Tordre leurs cheveux verts et longs jusqu'à leurs pieds

Debout chantez plus haut en dansant une ronde
Que je n'entende plus le chant du batelier
Et mettez près de moi toutes les filles blondes
Au regard immobile aux nattes repliées

Le Rhin le Rhin est ivre où les vignes se mirent
Tout l'or des nuits tombe en tremblant s'y refléter
La voix chante toujours à en râle-mourir
Ces fées aux cheveux verts qui incantent l'été

Mon verre s'est brisé comme un éclat de rire

Alcools

Qu'est-ce qui se passe

Je monte la garde à la poudrière
Il y a un chien très gentil dans la guérite
Il y a des lapins qui détalent dans la garrigue
Il y a des blessés dans la salle de garde

Rhenish Night

My glass is full of a wine that wavers like a flame
Listen to the slow chantey the boatman sings
Who tells of having seen seven women in the moonlight
Twisting down to their feet their long green hair

Stand up sing louder and dance in a round
Deafen the boatman's song
And gather about me all the blondes there are
With their steady gaze and their hair up in braids

The Rhine the Rhine is drunk where the vineyards glisten
The gold of the nights falls trembling reflecting itself
In the throes of death the voice still sings
Of the green-haired nymphs who enchant the summer

My glass shattered like a burst of laughter

                                                    S.G.

What's Happening

I stand guard over the munitions dump
There is a very nice dog in the sentry-box
There are rabbits that scamper about in the sand
There are wounded men in the guard room

Il y a un fonctionnaire brigadier qui pince le nez aux ronfleurs
Il y a une route en corniche qui domine de belles vallées
Pleines d'arbres en fleurs qui colorent le printemps
Il y a des vieillards qui discutent dans les cafés
Il y a une infirmière qui pense à moi au chevet de son blessé
Il y a de grands vaisseaux sur la mer déchaînée
Il y a mon cœur qui bat comme le chef d'orchestre
Il y a des Zeppelins qui passent au-dessus de la maison de ma
     mère
Il y a une femme qui prend le train à Baccarat
Il y a des artilleurs qui sucent des bonbons acidulés
Il y a des alpins qui campent sous des marabouts
Il y a une batterie de 90 qui tire au loin
Il y a tant d'amis qui meurent au loin

                    Le Guetteur mélancolique

Merci bien cher André de ta lettre au crayon
Ne suis pas amoureux et j'ai de ses nouvelles
Nous ne savons rien d'elle et notre opinion
Est donc sans importance
                  Et sur les Dardanelles
Parle-m'en car je crois que j'y vais de ce pas
Avant qu'il soit longtemps ou bien au bois Le Prêtre
Mourir au nord au sud c'est le même trépas
Mais au ciel d'Orient on souffre moins peut-être

Ah! que je voudrais voir tes poèmes secrets
Pour Vallette je fais ma *Vie anecdotique*

There is an N.C.O who pinches the noses of snorers
There is a coast road that overlooks beautiful valleys
Full of trees in bloom that color the spring
There are old men who argue in the cafés
There is a nurse who thinks of me as she stands next to her
    patient
There are great ships on the turbulent seas
There is my heart beating like an orchestra conductor
There are Zeppelins that pass over my mother's house
There is a woman who takes the train at Baccarat
There are riflemen who suck on sour candies
There are Alpine troops sleeping in their tents
There is a 90mm battery firing in the distance
There are so many friends dying in the distance

                          S.G.

Thanks a lot dear André for your pencilled letter
Am not in love and I've got news of her
Nobody knows anything about her and consequently
Our opinion does not count
                  Tell me about
The Dardanelles because I think I'm heading there
In the near future or else to the Woods of Le Prêtre
To die in the North or the South it's the same death
But perhaps it's less painful under the Eastern sky

I'd really like to see your secret poems
I'm writing a *Gossip Column* for Vallette

Mais que ne sommes-nous *à l'ombre des forê*ts
Devisant et fumant Au diable la tactique
Qu'il revienne le temps des courses en auto
Je conduis un canon sous un ciel sans nuage
Et je te dois toujours ma promise photo
Tu m'y verras conduire un superbe attelage

Poèmes épistolaires

But why aren't we *in the shadow of the forests*
Chatting and smoking To hell with tactics
God! for those good old days of car racing
I'm driving a cannon under a cloudless sky
And I haven't forgotten the photograph I promised you
In it you'll see me driving a magnificent pair of horses

S.G.

Jules Supervielle ✠✠✠ 1884-1960

Three of the thirteen poets represented in this book, Lau-
tréamont, Laforgue, and Supervielle, were born in Mon-
tevideo, Uruguay. Although all of them were French by inher-
itance, and sooner or later by adoption, there must have been
something particularly salutary for poetry in that South
American climate. The three poets, Laforgue to a lesser degree,
have in common a sense of space, an attraction toward the
great expanses of the ocean, or, in Supervielle, the pampas.
While Lautréamont made the cosmos a playground for the hor-
rendous freedom of Maldoror, Supervielle would evoke the life
and death of the Earth, in order to bring adequate intensity to
the fact that the world is blessed with something called a gold-
finch. He can make one raindrop represent the poignant im-
passe which is death. Elsewhere, death gives a special illumi-
nation to life; no poems offer a more convincing experience of
the particular joy of the physical, the mere fact of having a tan-
gible body in a tangible world. As for the mind which cele-
brates or mourns this joy, the stars may depend on thought for
their very existence, but in one of Supervielle's most impres-
sive stories, "L'Enfant de la haute mer," a thought "of terrible
intensity" condemns a child to perpetual solitude, visible only
to the ocean whose sympathy cannot even offer death to her.
Supervielle is a poet of tenderness and simplicity, but the
reader, passing through his works as through a garden, may
find himself confronting terrifying revelations.

P.T.

Un Poète

Je ne vais pas toujours seul au fond de moi-même
Et j'entraîne avec moi plus d'un être vivant.
Ceux qui seront entrés dans mes froides cavernes
Sont-ils sûrs d'en sortir, même pour un moment?
J'entasse dans ma nuit, comme un vaisseau qui sombre,
Pêle-mêle, les passagers et les marins,
Et j'éteins la lumière aux yeux, dans les cabines,
Je me fais des amis des grandes profondeurs.

Les Amis inconnus

La Demeure entourée

Le corps de la montagne hésite à ma fenêtre:
"Comment peut-on entrer si l'on est la montagne,
Si l'on est en hauteur, avec roches, cailloux,
Un morceau de la Terre, altéré par le Ciel?"
Le feuillage des bois entoure ma maison:
"Les bois ont-ils leur mot à dire là-dedans?
Notre monde branchu, notre monde feuillu
Que peut-il dans la chambre où siège ce lit blanc,
Près de ce chandelier qui brûle par le haut,
Et devant cette fleur qui trempe dans un verre?
Que peut-il pour cet homme et son bras replié,
Cette main écrivant entre ces quatre murs?

A Poet

I don't always go alone to the bottom of my self;
Quite often living captives keep me company.
Those who have stepped inside my cold caverns,
Are they sure that they can ever leave again?
Like a sinking ship I pile up in my night
Pell-mell all the passengers and sailors,
Then I turn off every cabin's light;
The great depths will soon become my friends.

P.T.

The House Surrounded

The mountain hesitates outside my window:
"How can I come in, if I am a mountain,
Extending as I do upwards, with rocks and pebbles,
A piece of the Earth, and thirsting under the Sky?"
The foliage of woods surrounds my house:
"What have the woods to say about all this?
Our world spread out in branches, leafy world,
What can it do in that room with its white bed,
Where a candlestick is burning at its peak,
Close to that flower sipping from a glass?
What can it do for that man who leans on his arm,
For a hand which writes in the shelter of four walls?

Prenons avis de nos racines délicates,
Il ne nous a pas vus, il cherche au fond de lui
Des arbres différents qui comprennent sa langue.''
Et la rivière dit: ''Je ne veux rien savoir,
Je coule pour moi seule et j'ignore les hommes.
Je ne suis jamais là où l'on croit me trouver
Et vais me devançant, crainte de m'attarder.
Tant pis pour ces gens-là qui s'en vont sur leurs jambes,
Ils partent, et toujours reviennent sur leurs pas.''
Mais l'étoile se dit: ''Je tremble au bout d'un fil,
Si nul ne pense à moi je cesse d'exister.''

Les Amis inconnus

Perdu parmi les pas et les ruines des astres
Et porté sur l'abîme où s'engouffre le ciel,
J'entends le souffle en moi des étoiles en marche
Au fond d'un cœur, hélas, que je sais éternel.
J'arrive de la Terre avec ma charge humaine
D'espoirs pris de panique et d'abrupts souvenirs,
Mais que faire en plein ciel d'un cœur qui se démène
Comme sous le soleil et n'a pas su mourir.
Avez-vous vu mes yeux errer dans ces parages
Où le loin et le près ignorent les rivages?
Aveugle sans bâton et sans force et sans foi,
Je cherche un corps, celui que j'avais autrefois.
Puissé-je préserver des avides espaces
Mes souvenirs rôdant autour de la maison,
Les visages chéris et ma pauvre raison
D'où je me surveillais comme d'une terrasse.

Let us take counsel from our fragile roots:
He hasn't seen us, he searches within himself
For trees which understand what he has to say."
And the river: "This is no concern of mine;
For myself alone I flow and know nothing of men.
Wherever they find me I have already gone,
Always ahead of myself, I fear to linger.
Who cares for people who walk away on their legs—
They leave, and they retrace their steps each time."
But the star says, "Trembling I hang by a thread;
I cease to exist if no one thinks of me."

                                                    P.T.

Lost among the footsteps and ruins of stars
And drawn into the gulf which devours the sky,
I can hear the breathing of stars on the march
In the depths of my, alas, eternal heart.
I have come here from Earth with all my human freight
Of panic-stricken hopes and abrupt memories—
What use in the sky is a heart which carries on
As if still under the sun, and can't learn how to die.
Have you seen my eyes wandering in this place
Where the near and far alike refuse all shore?
Blind and without a cane or strength or faith,
I seek a body, the one I had before.
If only I could keep from avid space
The memories prowling still around my home,
The faces dear to me, and, like a terrace,
Reason from which I overlooked myself.

Que je sauve du moins ce vacillant trésor
Comme un chien aux longs poils sous l'écume marine
Qui tient entre ses dents son petit presque mort.
Mais voici s'avancer l'écume des abîmes . . .
L'univers où je suis pousse un cruel soupir
Et la gorge du ciel profonde se soulève.
Puisque tout me rejette ici, même le rêve,
Ces lieux sans terre, à quoi pourraient-ils consentir?

Ah! même dans la mort je souffre d'insomnies,
Je veux de l'éternel faire un peu de présent,
Je me sens encor vert pour entrer au néant
Et chante mal dans l'universelle harmonie.
Comment renoncerais-je à tant de souvenirs
Quand l'esprit encombré d'invisibles bagages
Je suis plus affairé dans la mort qu'en voyage
Et je flotte au lieu de sombrer dans le mourir.
Les quatre bouts de bois qui me tenaient sous terre
N'empêchaient pas le ciel d'entrer au cimetière.
Le monde me devient un immense radeau
Où l'âme va et vient sans trouver son niveau.
Tout se relève avec la pierre de la tombe,
Notre premier regard délivre cent colombes.
Pour qui ne possédait que sa longueur de bois,
Les arbres, c'est déjà le plus bel au-delà.

1939–1945

Prophétie

à Jean Cassou
Un jour la Terre ne sera

Let me save at least this vacillating treasure,
Like a long-haired dog who grips between his jaws
His little one almost dead, and fights the seafoam.
But closer now the foam of the abyss . . .
The universe around me utters a cruel sigh,
And the deep gorge of the sky rises.
Since all rejects me here, and even dream,
What promise holds this realm, empty of land?

Ah! even in death I have trouble sleeping,
I want to make forever a bit of now;
I'm still too young to be part of nothingness,
Off key among the cosmic harmonies.
How can I renounce those memories
When so much invisible luggage on my mind
Keeps me busier now than when I traveled,
And I float on death instead of sinking down.
Four planks of wood held me under the ground,
But the cemetery still let in the sky.
On the world, now an immense raft, my soul
Goes back and forth, but never quite in balance.
All rises once again as does the tombstone,
A hundred doves are freed by our first glance.
I had only my length in wood to call my own;
Beyond is splendor in the trees alone.

P.T.

Prophecy

To Jean Cassou
Some day the Earth will be only

Qu'un aveugle espace qui tourne
Confondant la nuit et le jour.
Sous le ciel immense des Andes
Elle n'aura plus de montagnes,
Même pas un petit ravin.

De toutes les maisons du monde
Ne durera plus qu'un balcon
Et de l'humaine mappemonde
Une tristesse sans plafond.
De feu l'Océan Atlantique
Un petit goût salé dans l'air,
Un poisson volant et magique
Qui ne saura rien de la mer.

D'un coupé de mil-neuf-cent-cinq
(Les quatre roues et nul chemin!)
Trois jeunes filles de l'époque
Restées à l'état de vapeur
Regarderont par la portière
Pensant que Paris n'est pas loin
Et ne sentiront que l'odeur
Du ciel qui vous prend à la gorge.

A la place de la forêt
Un chant d'oiseau s'élèvera
Que nul ne pourra situer,
Ni préférer, ni même entendre,
Sauf Dieu qui, lui, l'écoutera
Disant: ''C'est un chardonneret.''

Gravitations

A blind space turning
Mingling night and day.
The vast sky of the Andes
Will float above no mountains,
Not even a small ravine.

All the world's houses will vanish
Except for one balcony,
A boundless grief will stand
For human geography.
And from the late Atlantic
A taste of salt in the air,
A fish flying and magic,
Ignorant of the sea.

In a nineteen-five coupé
(Four wheels without a road!)
Three young girls of the day
Who stayed behind as mist
Will look out the window quite sure
That Paris can't be far,
And all they will find is the odor
Of sky that sticks in your throat.

Out of the absent forest
Will rise the song of a bird
No one at all can place,
Prefer, or even hear
Except God—He will listen
And say, "That's a goldfinch."

P.T.

Le Regret de la Terre

Un jour, quand nous dirons: "C'était le temps du soleil,
Vous souvenez-vous, il éclairait la moindre ramille,
Et aussi bien la femme âgée que la jeune fille étonnée,
Il savait donner leur couleur aux objets dès qu'il se posait,
Il suivait le cheval coureur et s'arrêtait avec lui,
C'était le temps inoubliable où nous étions sur la Terre,
Où cela faisait du bruit de faire tomber quelque chose,
Nous regardions alentour avec nos yeux connaisseurs,
Nos oreilles comprenaient toutes les nuances de l'air
Et lorsque le pas de l'ami s'avançait nous le savions,
Nous ramassions aussi bien une fleur qu'un caillou poli,
Le temps où nous ne pouvions attraper la fumée,
Ah! c'est tout ce que nos mains sauraient saisir maintenant."

Les Amis inconnus

La Goutte de Pluie

Dieu parle:
   Je cherche une goutte de pluie
   Qui vient de tomber dans la mer.
   Dans sa rapide verticale
   Elle luisait plus que les autres
   Car seule entre les autres gouttes
   Elle eut la force de comprendre

Regretting the Earth

Some day we will be saying, "That was the time of the sun,
Do you remember its light fell on the slightest twig,
The elderly woman or young astonished girl,
As soon as it touched it gave their color to things,
Kept pace with the galloping horse and stopped when he did,
That unforgettable time when we were still on Earth
Where if we dropped something it made a noise,
We would look around us with our knowing eyes,
And our ears would catch the slightest nuance in the air,
When the footsteps of a friend approached, we knew,
We used to gather flowers or smooth pebbles,
At that time we never could take hold of smoke,
Ah! What else can our hands do for us now?"

                                                          P.T.

The Raindrop

God speaks:
    I am looking for a raindrop
    Just fallen into the sea.
    Gleaming the length of its plummet
    More than any of the others,
    This raindrop alone among them
    Had the power to understand

Que, très douce dans l'eau salée,
Elle allait se perdre à jamais.
Alors je cherche dans la mer
Et sur les vagues, alertées,
Je cherche pour faire plaisir
A ce fragile souvenir
Dont je suis seul dépositaire.
Mais j'ai beau faire, il est des choses
Où Dieu même ne peut plus rien
Malgré sa bonne volonté
Et l'assistance sans paroles
Du ciel, des vagues et de l'air.

La Fable du monde

That very sweet in salt water
It would soon be lost forever.
And so I look in the sea
And on the now vigilant waves,
Trying at least to do something
For that fragile memory
Which entrusted itself to my care.
But it's no use; there are things
Which cannot be helped, even
By God, despite His good will
And the wordless interventions
Of the sky, the waves, and the air.

                                              P.T.

Pierre Reverdy ✤✤✤ 1889-1960

Much that has been labelled surrealistic in Reverdy's work is equally fundamental to Rimbaud's: the belief that a poem must attack, or at least elude, the limiting procedures of reason, that a poem is a journey which creates its own destination, that the significance of a poem will be in its own words exclusively. Reverdy's poems, by their cohesive organization and their impersonal quality, are closer to *Illuminations* than to the surrealists' often discursive experiments. Both poets were men of faith denied the assistance of God, and both sought the absolute through the things of this world, channelled into words. Reverdy's temperament, however, is far less violent than Rimbaud's, his intensity totally different in effect. It is as if their poems generated similar electrical charges in opposite directions: Rimbaud's radiating outward from a dense core, Reverdy's seeming to attract, and hold, the vastness of space. His isolated images, verbal gestures, are like the widely separated stars of a constellation, simultaneously giving a coherence to space and setting their own brilliance against its dark background. With an unprecedented economy of means, Reverdy condenses the major experiences of life into delicate abstractions, strong enough, for all their discretion, to evoke the ultimate death, the last sounds of the Earth when there will be no ears to hear them, or the perpetual uncertainties of life, its probably irrelevant juxtapositions, and its basic quality of being always and everywhere, in spite of everything, *une fête,* a celebration.

P.T.

Allégresse

L'air sent la mer
L'hiver à une pareille altitude m'effraie
On ne sait où naissent les vents
Ni quelle direction ils prennent
La maison tangue comme un bateau
Quelle main nous balance

Au cri poussé au dehors je sortis
Pour voir
Une femme se noyait
Une femme inconnue
Je lui tendis la main
Je la sauvai

Après lui avoir dit mon nom
Qu'elle ne connaissait pas
Je la mis à sécher à l'endroit le plus chaud
Je la vis revenir à la vie et embellir
Puis comme la chaleur augmentait
Elle disparut

Les Ardoises du toit

Joyous

The air smells of the sea
Winter at such an altitude frightens me
Who knows where the winds are born
Or what will be their direction
The house pitches like a ship
We are balanced on what hand

Hearing a cry I went outside
To look
A woman was drowning
A stranger
I stretched out my hand
I saved her

After telling her my name
Which she didn't know
I set her to dry in the warmest place
I saw her return more beautiful to life
Then as the heat was increasing
She disappeared

                                        P.T.

Les Ardoises du toit

Sur chaque ardoise
                    qui glissait du toit
                            on
                    avait écrit
                                    un poème

La gouttière est bordée de diamants
                        les oiseaux les boivent
                            Les Ardoises du toit

Son de cloche

            Tout s'est éteint
Le vent passe en chantant
                    Et les arbres frissonnent
Les animaux sont morts
Il n'y a plus personne
                            Regarde
Les étoiles ont cessé de briller
                    La terre ne tourne plus
Une tête s'est inclinée
                    Les cheveux balayant la nuit
Le dernier clocher resté debout
                    Sonne minuit
                            Les Ardoises du toit

The Roof Slates

On every slate
              sliding from the roof
                        someone
              had written
                              a poem

The gutter is rimmed with diamonds
                        the birds drink them
                                        P.T.

Sound of a Bell

        All the lights are out
The wind passes singing
                  And the trees shiver
The animals are dead
There is no one left
                  Look
The stars are not shining now
            Or the Earth turning
A head has bowed
              hair sweeps the night
The last bell tower upright
            Strikes midnight
                                P.T.

Miracle

Tête penchée
                    Cils recourbés
Bouche muette
Les lampes se sont allumées
Il n'y a plus qu'un nom
                    Que l'on a oublié
La porte se serait ouverte
Et je n'oserais pas entrer
                    Tout ce qui se passe derrière

On parle
                    Et je peux écouter

Mon sort était en jeu dans la pièce à côté

Les Ardoises du toit

Route

Sur le seuil personne
                    Ou ton ombre
Un souvenir qui resterait
La route passe
          Et les arbres parlent plus près
Qu'y a-t-il derrière

Miracle

Bowed head
                Upturned eyelashes
Mute mouth
The lamps have been lighted
The only thing left is a name
                        They have forgotten
Were the door to open
I would not dare go in
                All that is happening behind

They are talking
                And I can listen

My future was at stake in the next room

                                        P.T.

Route

On the threshold no one
                Or your shadow
A lingering memory
The route passes by
        And the trees come closer as they talk
What is there behind

Un mur
des voix
Les nuages qui s'élevèrent
Au moment où je passais là
Et tout le long une barrière
Où sont ceux qui n'entreront pas

Les Ardoises du toit

Dans Les Champs ou sur la colline

Non
Le personnage historique
Et là le soleil s'arrêtait
C'était un homme qui passait
Le cheval si maigre
Qu'aucune ombre ne poursuivait

La neige serait étonnante
Tout était blanc à quelques pas

Sur tous les animaux qui moururent de froid
Entre les arbres et la mer
L'eau clapotante
Le ciel amer
Resté seul entre les paysans et la lune
Le soir qui descendait devait venir de loin
Lentement la chanson dépassait nos mémoires
Fallait-il sourire ou y croire
On attendait
On regardait
C'est à tout ce qui se passait ailleurs que l'on pensait

Les Ardoises du toit

           A wall
                 voices
The clouds that lifted
Just as I was passing
And all along a barrier
          those who shall not enter

                            P.T.

In the Fields or on the Hill

          No
           Historical figure
And there the sun was coming to a stop
It was a man passing by
          His horse so thin
          Not the slightest shadow followed

The snow would be enormous
           A few steps away and everything was white

Over all the animals who died of cold
          Between the trees and the sea
Quick lapping water
          The bitter sky
  Left alone between the peasants and the moon
The evening was coming down and from far away
Slowly the song was leaving our memories behind
          Were we supposed to smile or believe it
     We were waiting
          And watching
Everything happening elsewhere was in our minds.

                            P.T.

Cabaret

Ce bois
Et une auberge où tout le monde fume
On ne voit plus rien les gens s'entassent
Reconnais-tu cet homme à son chapeau à plumes
Personne n'est venu pour voir ce qui se passe
Toute liberté acquise maîtresse du lieu
à la rumeur du sens commun qui se révolte
qui rirait en chantant des louanges à Dieu
le vorace y prépare sa prochaine récolte
Et l'heure de ton sort s'ébat dans la campagne
Un bruit distinct
malgré le sang lourd qui bourdonne du souvenir
revint comme j'allais guérir
Et l'être inespéré qui parfois nous pardonne
en voyant qui j'étais m'empêcha de sortir
Bientôt il se passa des choses extraordinaires
que les habitués du lieu ne semblent plus apercevoir
Il est encore temps de baisser vos paupières
puisque vous n'avez pas la force de tout voir
Le coin le plus propice nous était réservé entre la cheminée et
    la fenêtre
Le chien qui couche dans les cendres s'est éveillé
Le chat qui sait fumer ronronne devant l'âtre
Personne n'a soif
Les liqueurs ont un sale goût de bouchon
Quel chapeau a recouvert ton front
Chapeau pointu chapeau terrible
en le quittant tes idées s'en iront

Cabaret

These woods
And a tavern where everybody smokes
You can't see anything anymore people are on top of each other
Do you recognize that man with the feathers in his hat
Nobody came to see what is going on
Complete liberty mistress of the place
to the din of common sense revolting
that would laugh singing God's praises
there the voracious is preparing his next harvest
And the hour of your destiny gambols in the countryside
A clear noise
despite the heavy blood humming with memories
came back as I was recovering
And the unhoped-for being who sometimes forgives us
seeing who I was stopped me from leaving
Soon extraordinary things occurred
that the regular customers seem no longer to be aware of
There is still time for you to lower your eyelids
since you don't have enough strengh to see everything
The most propitious corner was reserved for us between the
        fireplace and the window
The dog asleep in the ashes has awakened
The cat who knows how to smoke purrs in front of the fire
Nobody is thirsty
The drinks have a lousy taste of cork
What hat covered your forehead
Pointed hat awful hat
when you take it off your ideas will fly away

Il ne restera plus de toi qu'un homme ridicule
Écoute le ruisseau qui pleure sa chanson
Et le vent dans les arbres du cimetière
Malgré la curiosité il faut que je t'emporte
en passant par la porte de derrière
Nous avons encore du chemin à parcourir
Et rien à faire là dedans
où tout le monde a l'air de retenir ses larmes

Cale-sèche

Chemin tournant

Il y a un terrible gris de poussière dans le temps
Un vent du sud avec de fortes ailes
Les échos sourds de l'eau dans le soir chavirant
Et dans la nuit mouillée qui jaillit du tournant des voix
      rugueuses qui se plaignent
Un goût de cendre sur la langue
Un bruit d'orgue dans les sentiers
Le navire du cœur qui tangue
Tous les désastres du métier

Quand les feux du désert s'éteignent un à un
Quand les yeux sont mouillés comme des brins d'herbe
Quand la rosée descend les pieds nus sur les feuilles
Le matin à peine levé
Il y a quelqu'un qui cherche
Une adresse perdue dans le chemin caché
Les astres dérouillés et les fleurs dégringolent

Only a ridiculous man will remain behind
Listen to the stream weeping its song
And the wind in the trees of the cemetery
Despite our curiosity I must take you with me
going out by the back door
We still have a ways to go
And nothing to do in there
where everyone seems to be holding back his tears
                                                    S.G.

Winding Road

There is a terrible greyness of dust in the air
A wind from the south with powerful wings
Muffled echoes of water in the evening about to capsize
And in the wet night that springs from the curve harsh voices
        complaining
A taste of ashes on the tongue
Organ sounds along the paths
The pitching ship of the heart
All the catastrophes of our occupation

When the desert fires go out one by one
When the eyes are as wet as blades of grass
When the dew's bare feet come down upon the leaves
The morning scarcely arisen
Someone is searching
The hidden road for a lost address
The stars brightened up and the flowers tumble down

A travers les branches cassées
Et le ruisseau obscur essuie ses lèvres molles à peine décollées
Quand le pas du marcheur sur le cadran qui compte règle le
     mouvement et pousse l'horizon
Tous les cris sont passés tous les temps se rencontrent
Et moi je marche au ciel les yeux dans les rayons
Il y a du bruit pour rien et des noms dans ma tête
Des visages vivants
                    Tout ce qui s'est passé au monde
Et cette fête
            Où j'ai perdu mon temps

Sources du vent

Through the broken branches
And the shadowy stream dries its soft, scarcely parted, lips
When someone walking over the dial that counts adjusts the
    movement and moves the horizon back
All the cries have passed the times all come together
And I walk in the sky my eyes on the paths of light
There are sounds to no purpose and names inside my head
Living faces
        Everything that has happened in the world
And that celebration
        Where I wasted my time

                                    P.T.

Paul Eluard ✠✠✠ 1895-1952

As a politically active poet, a member of the French Communist Party, and of the Resistance movement during World War Two, Paul Eluard, often in an apparently naive manner, tried to reconcile the differences that separated men. Goodness and fraternity, rather than recriminations and hostility, loom large in his work, reminding one of the humanitarian theme expressed by Victor Hugo in the nineteenth-century. But of equal importance to Eluard, one of the founders of the Surrealist movement, was the need to redefine the theme of love, making it the essential communion between men and women, an experience both mystical and sensual, particular and general. In this latter effort, Eluard associates himself with what is unquestionably one of the most dominant and fascinating subjects in all of French poetry. The facility with which he writes, the felicity of his imagery, the simplicity of his vocabulary, the rejection of all obscurity—these are the particular traits of his poetry. But if a reader is agreeably surprised, moved by certain passages, by their transparencies, he is, in fact, responding to a set of carefully adjusted signals that mark the poem and render its message effective. Foremost among the devices that assure such reactions are the figures of speech: metaphors and comparisons, hyperboles, personifications and metonymies. The poet is equally adept at moving from one verbal pattern to another, thereby breaking the reader's expectations. The appreciation of an Eluard poem thus requires a double and inseparable reading: thematic and stylistic.

S.G.

Nul

Ce qui se dit: J'ai traversé la rue pour ne plus être au soleil. Il fait trop chaud, même à l'ombre. Il y a la rue, quatre étages et ma fenêtre au soleil. Une casquette sur la tête, une casquette à la main, il vient me serrer la main. Voulez-vous ne pas crier comme ça, c'est de la folie!

Des aveugles invisibles préparent les linges du sommeil. La nuit, la lune et leur cœur se poursuivent.

À son tour un cri: "l'empreinte, l'empreinte, je ne vois plus l'empreinte. À la fin, je ne puis plus compter sur vous!"

Capitale de la douleur

L' Amoureuse

Elle est debout sur mes paupières
Et ses cheveux sont dans les miens,
Elle a la forme de mes mains,
Elle a la couleur de mes yeux,
Elle s'engloutit dans mon ombre
Comme une pierre sur le ciel.

Elle a toujours les yeux ouverts
Et ne me laisse pas dormir.

Nothing

What they're saying: I've crossed the street to get out of the sun. It's too hot even in the shade. There's the street, four flights up and my window in the sun. A cap on his head, a cap in his hand, he's coming to shake my hand. Would you please not yell like that, you must be mad!

Invisible blind men lay out the sheets for sleep. Night, the moon, and their hearts chase after each other.

And now his turn to yell: "The imprint, the imprint, I can't see the imprint anymore. It's perfectly evident, I can't count on you any more!"

S.G.

A Woman in Love

She stands on my eyelids
And her hair mingles with mine,
She has the shape of my hands,
She has the color of my eyes,
She disappears in my shadow
Like a stone against the sky.

She never closes her eyes
And never lets me sleep.

Ses rêves en pleine lumière
Font s'évaporer les soleils,
Me font rire, pleurer et rire,
Parler sans avoir rien à dire.

Mourir de ne pas mourir

Ta chevelure d'oranges dans le vide du monde
Dans le vide des vitres lourdes de silence
Et d'ombre où mes mains nues cherchent tous tes reflets.

La forme de ton cœur est chimérique
Et ton amour ressemble à mon désir perdu.
O soupirs d'ambre, rêves, regards.

Mais tu n'as pas toujours été avec moi. Ma mémoire
Est encore obscurcie de t'avoir vu venir
Et partir. Le temps se sert de mots comme l'amour.

Capitale de la douleur

La courbe de tes yeux fait le tour de mon cœur,
Un rond de danse et de douceur,
Auréole du temps, berceau nocturne et sûr,

Paul Eluard

Her dreams, in broad daylight
Make the suns evaporate,
Make me laugh, cry and laugh,
Speak with nothing to say.

S.G.

Your orange hair in the emptiness of the world
In the emptiness of the window panes, heavy with silence
And shadow, where my bare hands look for all your images.

The shape of your heart is fanciful
And your love resembles my lost desire.
O sighs of amber, dreams, and glances.

But you haven't always been with me. My memory
Is still darkened, having seen you come
And go. Time uses words like love.

S.G.

The curve of your eyes circles my heart,
A round of dance and gentleness,
Time's aureole, safe nocturnal cradle,

Et si je ne sais plus tout ce que j'ai vécu
C'est que tes yeux ne m'ont pas toujours vu.

Feuilles de jour et mousse de rosée,
Roseaux du vent, sourires parfumés,
Ailes couvrant le monde de lumière,
Bateaux chargés du ciel et de la mer,
Chasseurs des bruits et sources des couleurs

Parfums éclos d'une couvée d'aurores
Qui gît toujours sur la paille des astres,
Comme le jour dépend de l'innocence
Le monde entier dépend de tes yeux purs
Et tout mon sang coule dans leurs regards.

Capitale de la douleur

Le front aux vitres comme font les veilleurs de chagrin
Ciel dont j'ai dépassé la nuit
Plaines toutes petites dans mes mains ouvertes
Dans leur double horizon inerte indifférent
Le front aux vitres comme font les veilleurs de chagrin
Je te cherche par delà l'attente
Par delà moi-même
Et je ne sais plus tant je t'aime
Lequel de nous deux est absent.

L'Amour la poésie

Paul Eluard

And if I don't remember all that I have lived
Blame your eyes that haven't always seen me.

Leaves of day and froth of dew,
Reeds of the wind, perfumed smiles,
Wings spreading light over the world,
Boats laden with the sky and the sea,
Hunters of noises and springs of colors

Perfumes bursting from a brood of dawns
Always lying on a mat of stars,
As the day depends on innocence
The whole world depends on your clear eyes
And all my blood flows within their gaze.

                                                        S.G.

My forehead on window panes like watchers of sorrow
Sky whose night I have left behind
Plains very small in my open hands
In their double horizon inert indifferent
My forehead on window panes like watchers of sorrow
I look for you beyond expectation
Beyond myself
And I don't know anymore I love you so much
Which one of us is absent.

                                                        S.G.

Printemps

Il y a sur la plage quelques flaques d'eau
Il y a dans les bois des arbres fous d'oiseaux
La neige fond dans la montagne
Les branches des pommiers brillent de tant de fleurs
Que le pâle soleil recule

C'est par un soir d'hiver dans un monde très dur
Que je vis ce printemps près de toi l'innocente
Il n'y a pas de nuit pour nous
Rien de ce qui périt n'a de prise sur toi
Et tu ne veux pas avoir froid

Notre printemps est un printemps qui a raison.
Capitale de la douleur

À Pablo Picasso

I

Bonne journée j'ai revu qui je n'oublie pas
Qui je n'oublierai jamais
Et des femmes fugaces dont les yeux
Me faisaient une haie d'honneur
Elles s'enveloppèrent dans leurs sourires

Spring

There are puddles on the beach
In the forests there are trees wild with birds
Snow melts on the mountain
The branches of the apple-trees shine with so many flowers
That the pale sun retreats

It was a winter evening in a very harsh world
That I saw this spring next to you, innocent one
There is no night for us
Nothing that perishes has a hold on you
And you do not want to be cold

Our spring is a spring that is right.

                                                    S.G.

To Pablo Picasso

                    I
On a fine day I saw him again I haven't forgotten him
I shall never forget him
And fleeting women whose eyes
Formed an honor guard for me
They wrapped themselves in their smiles

Paul Eluard

Bonne journée j'ai vu mes amis sans soucis
Les hommes ne pesaient pas lourd
Un qui passait
Son ombre changée en souris
Fuyait dans le ruisseau

J'ai vu le ciel très grand
Le beau regard des gens privés de tout
Plage distante où personne n'aborde

Bonne journée journée qui commença mélancolique
Noire sous les arbres verts
Mais qui soudain trempée d'aurore
M'entra dans le cœur par surprise.

        II
Montrez-moi cet homme de toujours si doux
Qui disait les doigts font monter la terre
L'arc-en-ciel qui se noue le serpent qui roule
Le miroir de chair où perle un enfant
Et ces mains tranquilles qui vont leur chemin
Nues obéissantes réduisant l'espace
Chargées de désirs et d'images
L'une suivant l'autre aiguilles de la même horloge

Montrez-moi le ciel chargé de nuages
Répétant le monde enfoui sous mes paupières
Montrez-moi le ciel dans une seule étoile
Je vois bien la terre sans être ébloui
Les pierres obscures les herbes fantômes
Ces grands verres d'eau ces grands blocs d'ambre des
        paysages
Les jeux du feu et de la cendre
Les géographies solennelles des limites humaines

On a fine day I saw my friends without any worries
The men did not weigh much
One of them passing by
His shadow changed into a mouse
Ran off into a stream

I saw the sky stretch out wide
The splendid eyes of people who have nothing
Distant beaches where no one goes

On a fine day a day that began mournfully
Dark under the green trees
But which, all of a sudden, drenched in the dawn,
Entered my heart by surprise.

                    II
Show me that man who was always so kind
Who said fingers make the earth rise
The rainbow bends over itself the serpent rolls
The mirror of flesh where a child is beading
And those calm hands that go their way
Bare, obedient reducing space
Heavy with desires and images
One following the other hands on the same clock

Show me the sky heavy with clouds
Reflecting the world hidden beneath my eyelids
Show me the sky in a single star
I see the earth without being awed
Dark stones and ghostly weeds
Those large glasses of water those large blocks of amber
      landscapes
Games of fire and ashes
Solemn geographies of man's limitations

Paul Eluard

Montrez-moi aussi le corsage noir
Les cheveux tirés les yeux perdus
De ces filles noires et pures qui sont d'ici de passage et
    d'ailleurs à mon gré
Qui sont de fières portes dans les murs de cet été
D'étranges jarres sans liquide toutes en vertus
Inutilement faites pour des rapports simples
Montrez-moi ces secrets qui unissent leurs tempes
À ces palais absents qui font monter la terre.

Les Yeux fertiles

Show me also the dark figures
The hair brushed back eyes looking far away
Of those girls dark and pure who pass by on their way and
        besides much to my liking
Who are proud doors in the walls of this summer
Strange earthenware jars without liquids strong ones
Made for no reason for honest friendships
Show me those secrets that join their foreheads
To those empty palaces that make the earth rise.

                                               S.G.

Jean Follain ✤✤✤ 1903-71

Jean Follain's poems initially appear as snapshots. But as the reader explores the subject matter of the text, he becomes increasingly aware of the poet's own presence. Having denied the effectiveness of the discursive style, Follain concentrates on the brevity of the line whose power is heightened by a series of stylistic procedures that include syntactical reversals, unexpected rapprochements, breaking the semantic pattern with a striking word (mannikin, metaphysician); the reader even becomes aware of the scarcity of adjectives and the paucity of metaphors. These choices allow Follain to evoke his particular vision of a muted world where violence irrupts only to be reabsorbed into its natural setting. Many of his poems define this phenomenon: the taxidermist, the solitary walker who cuts down a spear of wheat, a fire that burns down a house. There is not only the event, there is also the poet's effort to fix a moment in the inexorable movement of time. "An insect stops/then goes on." The inhabitants of Follain's world—men, women, children, soldiers, artisans; animals, trees, fields, and hills—all function as indices of the cosmos. And yet, in this description of anguish, violence, and the passage of time, certain human emotions come to the fore: "hand in hand/two brothers . . ." The poet's gentler, more optimistic perspective comes to prevail.

S.G.

L'Empailleur d'oiseaux

L'empailleur s'était assis
devant les gorges roses
les ailes vertes ou mauves
de ses passereaux
rêvant à son amante
au corps si différent
parfois si près aussi
de celui des oiseaux
qu'il lui paraissait
très étrange
dans ses courbes et ses volumes
dans ses couleurs et ses parures
et dans ses ombres.

Exister

Écouter

Il y a ce qui rassure
et dort au creux de la chose
on l'écoute
dans la boucle du fleuve
dans la houille éclairant
de ses brasiers
le corps de la jeune fille

The Taxidermist

The taxidermist sat
in front of the rose throats
the wings green or mauve
of his sparrows
dreaming of his love
her body so different
and yet at times so like
that of the birds
that it seemed to him
very strange
in its curves and its volumes
in its colors and its ornaments
and in its shadows.
                                    S.G.

Listen

There is something reassuring
that sleeps at the heart of the matter
one can hear it
in the bend of the river
in the white coals lighting
with their fire
the body of the young girl

qui s'expose à la vie
dans la ramure et le jour clair
ou dans la nuit poignante.

Territoires

La Pomme rouge

Le Tintoret peignit sa fille morte
il passait des voitures au loin
le peintre est mort à son tour
de longs rails aujourd'hui
corsettent la terre
et la cisèlent
la Renaissance résiste
dans le clair-obscur des musées
les voix se muent
souvent même le silence
est comme épuisé
mais la pomme rouge demeure.

Territoires

Instant

Tant de visages sont
aux tournants
d'une lente existence

who welcomes life
in the boughs and the clear day
or in the poignant night.

                                    S.G.

The Red Apple

Tintoretto painted his dead daughter
cars were passing in the distance
the painter died in his turn
long rails today
corset the earth
and chisel it
the Renaissance resists
in the chiaroscuro of museums
voices change
often even silence
is almost exhausted
but the red apple remains.

                                    S.G.

Instant

So many faces are
at the turnings
of a slow existence

près des mêmes vitres
accueillantes au soleil.
C'est quand passe l'homme
sa poitrine solide, ses jambes alourdies
son sourire
que vibre le mieux
l'instant pur
du seul épi de blé
que sa main insoucieuse cueille
le faisant échapper à la faux.

Des Heures

Le Feu

De grands lierres s'étiraient
sur la maison grise
du métaphysicien
le feu y prit une nuit
éclairant la plaine rase
dans l'air flottèrent les cendres
dans l'odeur du foin brûlé
puis les cieux passèrent calmés
sur la ruine assaillie
par beaucoup d'enfants sans mère
qui sur ses brèches jouèrent
vêtus de haillons noircis
imaginant leur vie longue.

Des Heures

near the same windows
welcoming the sun.
It is when a man passes
his chest solid, his legs plodding
his smile
that pulses most strongly
the pure moment
of the single spear of wheat
which his careless hand picks
letting it escape the scythe.

                                    S.G.

Fire

Tall ivy stretched over
the grey house
of the metaphysician
one night it caught fire
lighting up the open fields
in the air ashes floated
in the smell of burned hay
then calm skies passed
over the ruin assaulted
by many orphans
who played in its breaches
dressed in blackened rags
imagining their lives long.

                                    S.G.

Accords

C'est la main dans la main
que doucement se sourient
deux frères en rébellion
il se traîne un fin nuage
sur le faubourg ocreux
aux fenêtres carrées
découpées dans ses murs
des visages regardent
s'aider des enfants graves
pour passer le ruisseau;
s'appuyant à l'arbre
sans feuilles et sans fruits
un prévoyant médite
sur le bord d'un abîme.

Des Heures

Boutique

Des hommes viennent chercher
avec un lent sourire
des paquets clos
parfois une bougie blanche
dans cette boutique austère
où pendent les sabots ornés

Agreements

Hand in hand
two brothers in rebellion
tenderly smile at each other
a thin cloud drags itself
over the ocherous suburb
at the square windows
cut out of its walls
faces are watching
solemn children help each other
across the stream;
leaning against a tree
without leaves or fruit
a cautious man meditates
on the edge of an abyss.

                                    S.G.

Shop

Men come to get
with a slow smile
wrapped packages
sometimes a white candle
in this austere shop
where ornate wooden shoes hang

leur voix calme:
"Y a-t-il du monde?"
Une femme vient enfin
les servir de ses mains
ayant cueilli l'herbe
au bord de ces chemins
que traverse si vite un lièvre
d'espèce commune.

Des Heures

Epoques

Que de main-d'œuvre
dans ces tressaillants rideaux
figurant des dieux
certains bourgeois acclamèrent
d'autres se terrèrent
entre des murs nus
un corps parfois s'offre
dans ces époques troublées
s'il y survit
il se peut qu'il ouvre la porte
donnant sur une cour glacée
où gît un mannequin
aux yeux bleus
couvert de terre argileuse.

D'Après tout

their voices quiet:
"Anybody here?"
A woman comes at last
to serve them with her hands
having gathered the grass
at the edge of these paths
so rapidly crossed by a hare
of the common sort.

S.G.

Epochs

So much workmanship
in these trembling curtains
depicting gods
some townspeople cheered
others hid in the earth
between bare walls
sometimes a shape appears
in these troubled times
if he survives them
he may open the door
on a frozen courtyard
where a blue-eyed
mannikin lies
covered with clay.

S.G.

Pensées d'Octobre

On aime bien
ce grand vin
que l'on boit solitaire
quand le soir illumine les collines cuivrées
plus un chasseur n'ajuste
les gibiers de la plaine
les sœurs de nos amis
apparaissent plus belles
il y a pourtant menace de guerre
un insecte s'arrête
puis repart.

Territoires

October Thoughts

One rather likes
this vintage wine
drunk in solitude
when the evening lights up the copper hills
no hunters are left who aim
at the game in the fields
our friends' sisters
look prettier
still there is the threat of war
an insect stops
then goes on.

                                        S.G.

Francis Ponge ✣✣✣ 1899-

For Francis Ponge, the proper study of poetry is language it-
self. Reacting vehemently against both romantic lyricism and
symbolist obscurities, he has long assumed that language
must be reclaimed, strengthened, and made adequate to its
original self-expressive purpose. Objects of the most insignifi-
cant kinds (a loaf of bread, for example) that have rarely been
the subject of poetry, are now used to found a new poetics; af-
fective langage having been abused through centuries of cli-
chéd expressions. The first step, then, is to reorient one's at-
tention, away from the self-indulgent preoccupations of men,
toward material objects that constitute the universe in which
we live. But objects in themselves are regarded as only a half-
way station by Ponge. For him, objects are the initial proving
grounds, the testing of one's new vocabulary. Clearly, objects
are not meant to replace lyrical evocations. Ponge assumes that
the poem, when it is stripped of all sentimentality and lexical
inaccuracies, becomes both a tonic and a didactic experience.
It establishes new rules, new ways of writing, new ways of
seeing the world, and thereby reclaims a part of the universe
left in the shadow ever since the Renaissance. As he declares
in *Les Mûres*, words lead neither to some objective "reality"
nor to some mystical point. The poem, ultimately, is an object
in itself. This is particularly clear in the long work *Le Pré*.
Here, Francis Ponge, giving infinite care to the etymology and
the phonemic qualities of words, describes linguistically (the
poet has no other choice) the fabrication of a meadow. Reality
does exist, the poet maintains, but it is wholly circumscribed
by the text itself. Ponge thus finds verbal equivalences that re-
establish the priority of language.

S.G.

Les Mûres

Aux buissons typographiques constitués par le poème sur une route qui ne mène hors des choses ni à l'esprit, certains fruits sont formés d'une agglomération de sphères qu'une goutte d'encre remplit.

Noirs, roses et kakis ensemble sur la grappe, ils offrent plutôt le spectacle d'une famille rogue à ses âges divers, qu'une tentation très vive à la cueillette.

Vue la disproportion des pépins à la pulpe les oiseaux les apprécient peu, si peu de chose au fond leur reste quand du bec à l'anus ils en sont traversés.

Mais le poète au cours de sa promenade professionnelle, en prend de la graine à raison: "Ainsi donc, se dit-il, réussissent en grand nombre les efforts patients d'une fleur très fragile quoique par un rébarbatif enchevêtrement de ronces défendue. Sans beaucoup d'autres qualités,—*mûres*, parfaitement elles sont mûres—comme aussi ce poème est fait.

Le Parti pris des choses

L'Huître

L'huître, de la grosseur d'un galet moyen, est d'une apparence plus rugueuse, d'une couleur moins unie, brillam-

Blackberries

On typographical bushes constituted by the poem along a road which leads neither beyond things nor to the spirit, certain fruits are formed by an agglomeration of spheres filled by a drop of ink.

Blacks, pinks, khakis, all on a cluster, they look more like members of an arrogant family of varying ages than a very lively temptation to pick them off.

Given the disproportion of the seeds to the pulp, birds find little to appreciate, so little in the end remains by the time it has traveled from the beak to the anus.

But the poet on his professional walk mulls this over in his mind: "Clearly," he says to himself," the patient efforts of a very delicate flower succeeds to a large extent although protected by a forbidding tangle of brambles. Lacking many other qualities—*blackberries* are perfectly ripe—the way this poem is ready."

S.G.

The Oyster

The oyster, the size of an average pebble, looks tougher, its color is less uniform, brilliantly whitish. It is a stubbornly

ment blanchâtre. C'est un monde opiniâtrement clos. Pourtant on peut l'ouvrir: il faut alors la tenir au creux d'un torchon, se servir d'un couteau ébréché et peu franc, s'y reprendre à plusieurs fois. Les doigts curieux s'y coupent, s'y cassent les ongles: c'est un travail grossier. Les coups qu'on lui porte marquent son enveloppe de ronds blancs, d'une sorte de halos.

A l'intérieur l'on trouve tout un monde, à boire et à manger: sous un *firmament* (à proprement parler) de nacre, les cieux d'en-dessus s'affaissent sur les cieux d'en-dessous, pour ne plus former qu'une mare, un sachet visqueux et verdâtre, qui flue et reflue à l'odeur et à la vue, frangé d'une dentelle noirâtre sur les bords.

Parfois très rare une formule perle à leur gosier de nacre, d'où l'on trouve aussitôt à s'orner.

Le Parti pris des choses

Le Pain

La surface du pain est merveilleuse d'abord à cause de cette impression quasi panoramique qu'elle donne: comme si l'on avait à sa disposition sous la main les Alpes, le Taurus ou la Cordillère des Andes.

Ainsi donc une masse amorphe en train d'éructer fut glissée pour nous dans le four stellaire, où durcissant elle s'est façonnée en vallées, crêtes, ondulations, crevasses . . . Et tous ces plans dès lors si nettement articulés, ces dalles minces où la lumière avec application couche ses feux,—sans un regard pour la mollesse ignoble sous-jacente.

closed world. And yet, it can be opened: one must then hold it in the hollow of a dish towel, use a jagged and rather tricky knife, repeat this many times. Curious fingers cut themselves on it, nails break on it: it's tough going. Hitting it that way leaves white circles, like halos, on its envelope.

Inside, one finds a whole world to drink and eat: under a nacreous *firmament* (strictly speaking), the heavens above recline on the heavens below and form a single pool, a viscous and greenish bag, that flows in and out when you smell it or look at it, fringed with blackish lace along the edges.

Sometimes, a very rare formula pearls in their nacreous throat, and right away you have an ornament.

S.G.

French Bread

The surface of a French bread is marvellous first of all because of that quasi-panoramic impression it gives: as if one had at one's fingertips the Alps, the Taurus, or the Andean Cordillera.

Thus an amorphous mass in the process of belching was pushed into the stellar oven for us, where, hardening, it has fashioned itself into valleys, peaks, undulations, crevasses . . . And, as of that moment, all those planes, so distinctly articulated, those thin tiles where the light carefully lays down its fires—without regard for the ignoble underlying softness.

Ce lâche et froid sous-sol que l'on nomme la mie a son tissu pareil à celui des éponges: feuilles ou fleurs y sont comme des soeurs siamoises soudées par tous les coudes à la fois. Lorsque le pain rassit ces fleurs fanent et se rétrécissent: elles se détachent alors les unes des autres, et la masse en devient friable . . .

Mais brisons-la: car le pain doit être dans notre bouche moins objet de respect que de consommation.

Le Parti pris des choses

La Barque

La barque tire sur sa longe, hoche le corps d'un pied sur l'autre, inquiète et têtue comme un jeune cheval.

Ce n'est pourtant qu'un assez grossier réceptacle, une cuiller de bois sans manche: mais, creusée et cintrée pour permettre une direction du pilote, elle semble avoir son idée, comme une main faisant le signe couci-couça.

Montée, elle adopte une attitude passive, file doux, est facile à mener. Si elle se cabre, c'est pour les besoins de la cause.

Lâchée seule, elle suit le courant et va, comme tout au monde, à sa perte tel un fétu.

Le Grand Recueil, iii

This loose and cold undercrust that one calls the white part has a texture similar to a sponge's: there, leaves or flowers, like Siamese twins, are fused together by all their elbows. In stale bread, these flowers wilt and shrink; they separate one from the other and the mass becomes easily crumbled . . .

But let's break it off here: after all, bread in our mouth must be eaten rather than respected.

S.G.

The Boat

The boat tugs on its rope, moves its weight from one foot to the other, restless and stubborn like a young horse.

It is only a rather crude receptacle, however, a wooden spoon without a handle: but hollowed and curved to let the pilot guide it, it seems to know where it's going, like a hand moving from side to side.

Mounted, it adopts a passive attitude, moves gently, is easy to lead. If it rears, it is all for the cause.

Left alone, ressembling a straw, it follows the current and goes, like everything else in the world, to its ruin.

S.G.

Le Pré

Que parfois la Nature, à notre réveil, nous propose
Ce à quoi justement nous étions disposés,
La louange aussitôt s'enfle dans notre gorge.
Nous croyons être au paradis.

Voilà comme il en fut du pré que je veux dire,
Qui fera mon propos d'aujourd'hui.

Parce qu'il s'y agit plus d'une façon d'être
Que d'un plat à nos yeux servi,
La parole y convient plutôt que la peinture
Qui n'y suffirait nullement.

Prendre un tube de vert, l'étaler sur la page,
Ce n'est pas faire un pré.
Ils naissent autrement.
Ils sourdent de la page.
Et encore faut-il que ce soit page brune.

Préparons donc la page où puisse aujourd'hui naître
Une vérité qui soit verte.

Parfois donc—ou mettons aussi bien par endroits—
Parfois, notre nature—
J'entends dire, d'un mot, la Nature sur notre planète
Et ce que, chaque jour, à notre réveil, nous sommes—
Parfois, notre nature nous a préparé(s) (à) un pré.

The Meadow

When at times Nature when we awaken proposes
Just what we were disposed to do,
Then praise immediately swells in our throat.
We think we are in paradise.

That is the way it was with the meadow I want to invoke
In my talk today.

Because it deals more with a way of being
Than a dish we've been asked to admire,
Words suit it better than paint
Which wouldn't do it justice at all.

Take a tube of green, spread it on the page,
That's not the way to make a meadow.
They are born differently.
They spring up from the page.
And then only from a brown page.

Let us then prepare the page upon which
A green truth may be born today.

At times, then—say, in certain places as well—
At times, our nature—
I mean by that, in a word, Nature on our planet
And what we are when we awake every morning—
At times, our nature has prepared us for a meadow.

Mais qu'est-ce, qui obstrue ainsi notre chemin?
Dans ce petit sous-bois mi-ombre mi-soleil,
Qui nous met ces bâtons dans les roues?
Pourquoi, dès notre issue en surplomb sur la page,
Dans ce seul paragraphe, tous ces scrupules?

Pourquoi donc, vu d'ici, ce fragment limité d'espace,
Tiré à quatre rochers ou à quatre haies d'aubépines,
Guère plus grand qu'un mouchoir,
Moraine des forêts, ondée de signe adverse,
Ce pré, surface amène, auréole des sources
Et de l'orage initial suite douce
En appel ou réponse unanime anonyme à la pluie,
Nous semble-t-il plus précieux soudain
Que le plus mince des tapis persans?

Fragile, mais non frangible,
La terre végétale y reprend parfois le dessus,
Où les petits sabots du poulain qui y galopa le marquèrent,
Ou le piétinement vers l'abreuvoir des bestiaux qui lentement
S'y précipitèrent . . .

Tandis qu'une longue théorie de promeneurs endimanchés,
        sans y
Salir du tout leurs souliers blancs, y procèdent
Au long du petit torrent, grossi, de noyade ou de perdition,
Pourquoi donc, dès l'abord, nous tient-il interdits?

Serions-nous donc déjà parvenus au naos,
Enfin au lieu sacré d'un petit déjeuné de raisons?
Nous voici, en tout cas, au cœur des pléonasmes
Et au seul niveau logique qui nous convient.

But what's this? Who thus blocks our way?
In this underbrush, half-shade, half-light,
Who throws the wrench in the works?
Why, when we come forth, bent over the page,
In this single paragraph, all these scruples?

Why then, seen from here, should this limited fragment of
  space,
Stretched out between four rocks or four hawthorn hedges,
Hardly larger than a handkerchief,
Forest moraine, showers falling adversely,
This meadow, pleasant surface, aureole of the springs
And the initial thunderstorm's gentle result
Calling or answering the rain unanimously or anonymously,
Suddenly appear to us more precious
Than the thinnest Persian rug?

Delicate but not brittle,
The vegetable earth sometimes regains the upper hand,
Where the young hoofs of the galloping colt marked it,
Or the steady trampling of the animals going to the trough
In a great rush . . .

While a long procession of Sunday strollers without
In any way soiling their white shoes, proceed
Along the little torrent, swollen by drownings or perdition,
Why then, from the outset, should we be held back?

Might we have already arrived at the naos,
Finally, to the sacred site of a light lunch of accommodations?
Here we are, in any case, at the heart of the pleonasms
And at the only logical level that suits us.

Ici tourne déjà le moulin à prières,
Sans la moindre idée de prosternation, d'ailleurs,
Car elle serait contraire aux verticalités de l'endroit.

Crase de paratus, selon les étymologistes latins,
Près de la roche et du ru,
Prêt à faucher ou à paître,
Préparé pour nous par la nature,
Pré, paré, pré, près, prêt.

Le pré gisant ici comme le participe passé par excellence
S'y révère aussi bien comme notre préfixe des préfixes,
Préfixe déjà dans préfixe, présent déjà dans présent.
Pas moyen de sortir de nos onomatopées originelles.
Il faut donc y rentrer.

Nul besoin, d'ailleurs, d'en sortir,
Leurs variations suffisant bien à rendre compte
De la merveilleusement fastidieuse
Monotonie et variété du monde,
Enfin, de sa perpétuité.

Encore faut-il les prononcer.
Parler. Et, peut-être, paraboler.
Toutes, les dire.
. . . .
(Ici doit intervenir un long passage, où, dans la manière
un peu de l'interminable séquence de clavecin solo du cin-
quième concerto brandebourgeois, c'est-à-dire de façon fas-
tidieuse et mécanique mais mécanisante à la fois, non telle-
ment de la musique que de la logique, raisonneuse, du bout
des lèvres, non de la poitrine ou du cœur, je tâcherai d'ex-
pliquer, je dis bien expliquer, deux ou trois choses, et d'abord
que si le pré, dans notre langue, représente une des plus im-

Here the prayer box has already begun to chatter,
Without in any way intending to kneel,
Because that would be contrary to the verticalities of the place.

Crasis of *paratus*, according to Latin etymologists.[1]
Near the rock and the water,
Ready to cut or to graze,
Prepared for us by nature,
Meadow, adorned, meadow, near, ready.[2]

The meadow lying here like the past participle *par excellence*
Reveres itself also as our prefix of prefixes,
Prefix already in prefix, present already in present.
No way of avoiding our initial onomatopoeias.
Therefore, let us accept them.

No need, moreover, to reject them,
Their variations are perfectly able to account
For the marvelously fastidious
Monotony and variety of the world,
In fact, its perpetuity.

But we must pronounce them.
Speak. And perhaps parabolate.
Say them, all.
. . . .

    (At this point, a long passage must be inserted in which, rather like the endless harpsichord solo of the Fifth Brandenburg Concerto, that is, in a fastidious and mechanical manner, mechanizing as well, not so much music as logic, reasoning, from the tip of the lips, not from the chest or the heart, I will try to explain, I repeat, explain two or three things, and first of all, that if the meadow, in our language, represents one of the most important and primordial logical

portantes et primordiales notions logiques qui soient, il en est
de même sur le plan physique (géophysique), car il s'agit en
vérité d'une métamorphose de l'eau, laquelle, au lieu de s'éva-
porer directement, à l'appel du feu, en nuages, choisit ici, se
liant à la terre et en passant par elle, c'est-à-dire par les restes
pétris du passé des trois règnes et en particulier par les granu-
lations les plus fines du minéral, réimprégnant en somme le
cendrier universel, de donner renaissance à la vie sous sa
forme la plus élémentaire, l'herbe: élémentarité-alimentarité.
Ce chapitre, qui sera *aussi* celui de la musique des prés, son-
nera de façon grêle et minutieuse, avec une quantité d'ap-
poggiatures, pour s'achever (s'il s'achève) en accelerando et
rinforzando à la fois, jusqu'à une sorte de roulement de ton-
nerre où nous nous réfugierons dans les bois. Mais la perfec-
tion de ce passage pourrait me demander quelques années en-
core. Quoi qu'il en soit . . .)

. . . .

        L'orage originel a longuement parlé.

. . . .

L'orage originel n'aura-t-il donc en nous si longuement grondé
Seulement pour qu'enfin
                —car il s'éloigne, n'occupant
                  plus que partiellement l'horizon
                  bas où il fulgure encore—
Parant au plus urgent, allant au plus pressé,
Nous sortions de ces bois,
Passions entre ces arbres et nos derniers scrupules,
Et, quittant tout portique et toutes colonnades,
Transportés tout à coup par une sorte d'enthousiasme paisible
En faveur d'une vérité, aujourd'hui, qui soit verte,
Nous nous trouvions bientôt alités de tout notre long sur ce
pré,
Dès longtemps préparé pour nous par la nature,
                —où n'avoir plus égard qu'au
                  ciel bleu.

notions imaginable, the same can also be truthfully said about it on the physical level (geophysical), because, in truth, it represents a metamorphosis of water which, instead of immediately evaporating, beckoned by fire, into clouds, chooses this place, becoming one with the earth and passing through it, that is, by the petrified remains of the past three reigns and in particular by the finest granulations of minerals, reimpregnating, in fact, the universal ashpit, to give birth to life in its most elementary form: grass elementarity—alimentation. This chapter, which will *also* be devoted to the music of the meadows, will sound high-pitched and detailed with many *appoggiaturas,* and then will conclude (if it can conclude) in a simultaneous *accelerando* and *rinforzando,* culminating in a roll of thunder, and at that moment, we will run for cover in the woods. But I might need a few more years to perfect this passage. Be that as it may . . .)

. . . .

The original thunderstorm spoke for a long time.

. . . .

Will the original thunderstorm only have boomed in us for
    such a long time
Just so that at last
                —because it moves away, now
                only partially occupying the lower horizon
                where it still flashes—
Warding off urgently, going as rapidly as possible,
We left the woods,
Passing through these trees and our last scruples,
And, leaving behind all porticos and all colonnades,
Carried away all of a sudden by a kind of peaceful enthusiasm
For a truth, today, which will be green,
We soon find ourselves stretched out on this meadow
Long ago prepared for us by nature,
                —now only attentive to
                the blue sky.

L'oiseau qui le survole en sens inverse de l'écriture
Nous rappelle au concret, et sa contradiction,
Accentuant du pré la note différentielle
Quant à tels près ou prêt, et au prai de prairie,
Sonne brève et aiguë comme une déchirure
Dans le ciel trop serein des significations.
C'est qu'aussi bien, le lieu de la longue palabre
Peut devenir celui de la décision.

Des deux pareils arrivés debout, l'un au moins,
Après un assaut croisé d'armes obliques,
Demeurera couché
D'abord dessus, puis dessous.

Voici donc, sur ce pré, l'occasion, comme il faut,
Prématurément, d'en finir.

Messieurs les typographes,
Placez donc ici, je vous prie, le trait final.
Puis, dessous, sans le moindre interligne, couchez mon nom,
Pris dans le bas-de-casse, naturellement,
                              Sauf les initiales, bien sûr,
                              Puisque ce sont aussi celles
                              Du Fenouil et de la Prêle
                              Quidemaincroîtrontdessus.

Francis Ponge.

Nouveau Recueil

The bird that flies over it in a direction opposite to the way we
     write
Brings us back to the fact, and its contradiction,
Accentuating the differential note of the meadow
When near or ready, and in the *prai* of prairie,
Rings quickly and sharply like a rent
In the sky too serene with meanings.
For it may just be that the site of these lengthy palavers,
Can become a dueling field.

Of the two who arrived, looking alike, and upright, one at
     least,
After an oblique crossing of the swords,
Will remain on his back,
First above, then below.

Here then, on this meadow, the moment has finally come,
To put an end to it, prematurely.

Typographers, sirs,
Would you kindly place the final line here.
Then, below, without any spacing, lay down my name,
In lower case, naturally,
                         Except for the initials, of course,
                         Since they also correspond
                         To the Fennel and Parsley
                         Thattomorrowwillgrowabove.

                         ———————————————

                                   Francis Ponge.

                                                        S.G.

[1] *Crasis,* Greek for *Krasis,* contraction of vowels; *Paratus,* Latin, prepared for.
[2] In French these are near homonyms.

Henri Michaux ✠✠✠ 1899–

Baudelaire saw the artist as isolated in a hostile, bourgeois society and yet playing in it a rôle of crucial importance. For Michaux, one hundred years later, the sense of alienation is more intimate and more profound. Michaux described himself as repelled, even in childhood, by food, odors, contacts, amusements; preferring immobility, dreams without images, without words. His body itself was ill-disposed, not making enough blood, and his blood "not mad about oxygen." Only two things pleased him before he was twelve: the discovery of the dictionary with its words undistorted by other people's sentences, and Latin, his "first journey." He escaped from his detested Belgian milieu by becoming a sailor, an occupation he left unwillingly in 1921—"the big window is closed"—but he continued to be a great traveller.

A reading of Lautréamont's *Maldoror* revived his long-forgotten need to express his experience in writing. He was not easily persuaded, believing that commitment to words would put an end to dreaming and to seclusion. The literary conventions, the very interest in literature for its own sake, seemed to him suspect. For Michaux, the principal functions of language are exorcism ("a prison displayed is not a prison") and exploration. Whether he has been charting the landscape of his own being, that of real or imaginary countries, or his drug-induced hallucinations, his subject has always been the experience of existing, his own experience, as an organism badly adapted to an inharmonious environment, surviving by virtue of humor and a desire to know strong enough to function as a will to live.

P.T.

La Simplicité

Ce qui a manqué surtout à ma vie jusqu'à présent, c'est la simplicité. Je commence à changer petit à petit.

Par exemple, maintenant, je sors toujours avec mon lit, et quand une femme me plaît, je la prends et couche avec aussitôt.

Si ses oreilles sont laides et grandes ou son nez, je les lui enlève avec ses vêtements et les mets sous le lit, qu' elle retrouve en partant; je ne garde que ce qui me plaît.

Si ses dessous gagneraient à être changés, je les change aussitôt. Ce sera mon cadeau. Si cependant je vois une autre femme plus plaisante qui passe, je m'excuse auprès de la première et la fais disparaître immédiatement.

Des personnes qui me connaissent prétendent que je ne suis pas capable de faire ce que je dis là, que je n'ai pas assez de tempérament. Je le croyais aussi, mais cela venait de ce que je ne faisais pas tout *comme il me plaisait*.

Maintenant, j'ai toujours de bonnes après-midi. (Le matin, je travaille.)

Mes Propriétés

Simplicity

Up to now, simplicity has truly been missing from my life. I'm beginning to change little by little.

For instance, now, I always go out with my bed, and when a woman pleases me, I grab her and sleep with her on the spot.

If her ears are large and ugly, or her nose, I remove them along with her clothing and put them under the bed for her to find when she goes; I only keep what I like.

If I can improve on her underwear, I change it on the spot. That's my gift. If, however, I see another woman passing by whom I prefer, I offer my apologies to the first and immediately make her disappear.

Some people who know me think that I'm incapable of doing what I've just said, that I don't have enough personality. I believed it too, but that was because I didn't do everything *the way I wanted to*.

Now, I always spend pleasant afternoons. (I work in the mornings.)

S.G.

La Paresse

L'âme adore nager.

Pour nager on s'étend sur le ventre. L'âme se déboîte et s'en va. Elle s'en va en nageant. (Si votre âme s'en va quand vous êtes debout, ou assis, ou les genoux ployés, ou les coudes, pour chaque position corporelle différente l'âme partira avec une démarche et une forme différentes, c'est ce que j'établirai plus tard.)

On parle souvent de voler. Ce n'est pas ça. C'est nager qu'elle fait. Et elle nage comme les serpents et les anguilles, jamais autrement.

Quantité de personnes ont ainsi une âme qui adore nager. On les appelle vulgairement des paresseux. Quand l'âme quitte le corps par le ventre pour nager, il se produit une telle libération de je ne sais quoi, c'est un abandon, une jouissance, un relâchement si intime . . .

L'âme s'en va nager dans la cage de l'escalier ou dans la rue suivant la timidité ou l'audace de l'homme, car toujours elle garde un fil d'elle à lui, et si ce fil se rompait (il est parfois très ténu, mais c'est une force effroyable qu'il faudrait pour rompre le fil) ce serait terrible pour eux (pour elle et pour lui).

Quand donc elle se trouve occupée à nager au loin, par ce simple fil qui lie l'homme à l'âme s'écoulent des volumes et

Laziness

The soul loves to swim.

To swim, you stretch out on your stomach. The soul disconnects and leaves you. It leaves you swimming. (If your soul leaves you when you're standing, or sitting, or with your knees crossed, or your elbows, for each different position of your body, the soul will go moving and holding itself in a different manner; I'll prove that later on.)

Flying is frequently mentioned. That's not it. Swimming is what it does. And it swims like serpents and eels, never in any other way.

A great number of people thus have a soul that loves to swim. In common parlance, we call them lazy. When the soul leaves the body through the stomach in order to swim, such an indescribable liberation occurs, it's such an indulgence, a pleasure, a secret relaxation . . .

The soul goes off swimming in the stairwell or in the street depending on the individual's timidity or courage, since he's always tied to it by a thread, and if that thread were to break (it is sometimes very thin, but you would have to be frightfully strong to break the thread), it would be terrible for them (for it and for him).

Consequently, when it's out swimming in the distance, just through this simple thread that joins man to the soul flow

des volumes d'une sorte de matière spirituelle, comme de la boue, comme du mercure, ou comme un gaz—jouissance sans fin.

C'est pourquoi le paresseux est indécrottable. Il ne changera jamais. C'est pourquoi aussi la paresse est la mère de tous les vices. Car qu'est-ce qui est plus égoïste que la paresse?

Elle a des fondements que l'orgueil n'a pas.

Mais les gens s'acharnent sur les paresseux.

Tandis qu'ils sont couchés, on les frappe, on leur jette de l'eau fraîche sur la tête, ils doivent vivement ramener leur âme. Ils vous regardent alors avec ce regard de haine, que l'on connaît bien, et qui se voit surtout chez les enfants.

Mes Propriétés

Clown

Un jour.

Un jour, bientôt peut-être.

Un jour j'arracherai l'ancre qui tient mon navire loin des mers.

Avec la sorte de courage qu'il faut pour être rien et rien que rien, je lâcherai ce qui paraissait m'être indissolublement proche.

volumes of a sort of spiritual matter, like mud, like mercury, or like gas—endless pleasure.

That's why you can't shake up a lazy man. He'll never change. That's also why laziness is the mother of all vices. After all, what's more selfish than laziness?

It's got a grounding that pride doesn't have.

But people are always jumping on the lazy.

While they're lying down, people hit them, throw cold water on their heads, they've got to bring back their souls in a hurry. At that moment, they look at you with that well-known look of hatred, and which can especially be seen on children.

S.G.

Clown

One day.

One day, soon perhaps.

One day I'll tear off the anchor that keeps my ship far away from the seas.

With a type of courage that's needed to be nothing and nothing but nothing, I'll let go of what seemed to have been indissolubly close to me.

Je le trancherai, je le renverserai, je le romprai, je le ferai dégringoler.

D'un coup dégorgeant ma misérable pudeur, mes misérables combinaisons et enchaînements "de fil en aiguille."

Vidé de l'abcès d'être quelqu'un, je boirai à nouveau l'espace nourricier.

À coups de ridicules, de déchéances (qu'est-ce que la déchéance?), par éclatement, par vide, par une totale dissipation-dérision-purgation, j'expulserai de moi la forme qu'on croyait si bien attachée, composée, coordonnée, assortie à mon entourage et à mes semblables, si dignes, si dignes, mes semblables.

Réduit à une humilité de catastrophe, à un nivellement parfait comme après une intense trouille.

Ramené au-dessous de toute mesure à mon rang réel, au rang infime que je ne sais quelle idée-ambition m'avait fait déserter.

Anéanti quant à la hauteur, quant à l'estime.

Perdu en un endroit lointain (ou même pas), sans nom, sans identité.

CLOWN, abattant dans la risée, dans le grotesque, dans l'esclaffement, le sens que contre toute lumière je m'étais fait de mon importance.

Je plongerai.
Sans bourse dans l'infini-esprit sous-jacent ouvert à tous,

I'll cut it down, flip it over, I'll break it, I'll make it tumble.

All at once throwing up my wretched sense of decency, my wretched and ponderous ways of thinking.

After I've cleaned out the abscess of being someone, I'll drink again of the nourishing space.

I'll suffer the pangs of ridicule, of ruin (what is ruin?) I'll burst, go through the void, through a total dissipation-derision-purgation, I'll expel from my body that form which everyone thought was so well tied together, ordered, coordinated, made to match that of my friends and my fellowmen, my so worthy, worthy fellowmen.

Reduced to the humility of catastrophe, a perfect leveling similar to the one that comes after being scared to death.

Brought back to the lowest possible position to my true place, to my minimal place that I had deserted for god-knows what idea-ambition.

My height and my esteem destroyed.

Lost in a far-away place (or not even that), without a name, without an identity.

CLOWN, laying low, among the jeers, the grotesque, the peals of laughter, the idea that I had of my own importance in the face of all evidence.

I'll dive in.
Penniless into the underlying infinite-soul open to everyone,

ouvert moi-même à une nouvelle et incroyable rosée
à force d'être nul
et ras . . .
et risible . . .

Peintures

"Je vous écris d'un pays lointain"

1

Nous n'avons ici, dit-elle, qu'un soleil par mois, et pour peu de temps. On se frotte les yeux des jours à l'avance. Mais en vain. Temps inexorable. Soleil n'arrive qu'à son heure.

Ensuite on a un monde de choses à faire, tant qu'il y a de la clarté, si bien qu'on a à peine le temps de se regarder un peu.

La contrariété pour nous dans la nuit, c'est quand il faut travailler, et il le faut: il naît des nains continuellement.

2

Quand on marche dans la campagne, lui confie-t-elle encore, il arrive que l'on rencontre sur son chemin des masses considérables. Ce sont des montagnes et il faut tôt ou tard se mettre à plier les genoux. Rien ne sert de résister, on ne pourrait plus avancer, même en se faisant du mal.

Ce n'est pas pour blesser que je le dis. Je pourrais dire d'autres choses, si je voulais vraiment blesser.

myself open to a new and unbelievable dew
by dint of having been nobody
and deflated . . .
and laughable . . .

S.G.

"I Am Writing to You from a Distant Land"

1

"Here we have only one sun a month," she says, "and not for long. Days in advance we start rubbing our eyes. But it doesn't help. Inexorable climate. A sun comes only in its own time.

Then we have a world of things to do, while the light lasts: we scarcely have time to take a look at each other.

What is vexing for us about night is when we have to work, and we do have to: dwarfs are born all the time."

2

"Sometimes," she confides to him further, "when we go walking in the country, we find large accumulations in our way. They are mountains, and sooner or later we have to begin bending our knees. It's useless to resist, there would be no way to move forward, even painfully.

I'm not saying this to hurt you. There are other things I could say, if I wanted to, that would hurt you very much."

3

L'aurore est grise ici, lui dit-elle encore. Il n'en fut pas toujours ainsi. Nous ne savons qui accuser.

Dans la nuit le bétail pousse de grands mugissements, longs et flûtés pour finir. On a de la compassion, mais que faire?

L'odeur des eucalyptus nous entoure: bienfait, sérénité, mais elle ne peut préserver de tout, ou bien pensez-vous qu'elle puisse réellement préserver de tout?

4

Je vous ajoute encore un mot, une question plutôt.

Est-ce que l'eau coule aussi dans votre pays? (je ne me souviens pas si vous me l'avez dit) et elle donne aussi des frissons, si c'est bien elle.

Est-ce que je l'aime? Je ne sais. On se sent si seule dedans quand elle est froide. C'est tout autre chose quand elle est chaude. Alors? Comment juger? Comment jugez-vous vous autres, dites-moi, quand vous parlez d'elle sans déguisement, à cœur ouvert?

5

Je vous écris du bout du monde. Il faut que vous le sachiez. Souvent les arbres tremblent. On recueille les feuilles. Elles ont un nombre fou de nervures. Mais à quoi bon? Plus rien entre elles et l'arbre, et nous nous dispersons gênées.

Est-ce que la vie sur terre ne pourrait pas se poursuivre sans vent? Ou faut-il que tout tremble, toujours, toujours?

3

"The dawn is grey here," she tells him further. "It wasn't always. We don't know whom to blame.

In the night the cattle make a deep, moaning sound, long and fluted at the end. Piteous, but what can we do?

We're surrounded by the fragrance of eucalyptus: a kindness, tranquility, but it can't protect us from every-thing—or do you think it really can protect us from every-thing?"

4

"I wanted to mention this, or rather ask you:

Does the water flow in your country too? (You may have told me this already.) And it can also make you shiver, if it's the real thing.

Am I fond of it? I don't know. In water that's cold one feels terribly alone. And quite different when it is warm. So how can I say? Tell me, what do you and your friends say of water, when you talk about it freely, with open hearts?"

5

"I am writing to you from the end of the world. I want you to know that. Often the trees tremble. We gather up their leaves. They have an incredible number of veins. But what's the use? Nothing's left between them and the trees, and we separate, feeling embarrassed.

Couldn't life on earth get along without the wind? Or does everything always, always, have to tremble?

Il y a aussi des remuements souterrains, et dans la maison comme des colères qui viendraient au-devant de vous, comme des êtres sévères qui voudraient arracher des confessions.

On ne voit rien, que ce qu'il importe si peu de voir. Rien, et cependant on tremble. Pourquoi?

6

Nous vivons toutes ici la gorge serrée. Savez-vous que, quoique très jeune, autrefois j'étais plus jeune encore, et mes compagnes pareillement. Qu'est-ce que cela signifie? Il y a là sûrement quelque chose d'affreux.

Et autrefois quand, comme je vous l'ai déjà dit, nous étions encore plus jeunes, nous avions peur. On eût profité de notre confusion. On nous eût dit: "Voilà, on vous enterre. Le moment est arrivé." Nous pensions, c'est vrai, nous pourrions aussi bien être enterrées ce soir, s'il est avéré que c'est le moment.

Et nous n'osions pas trop courir: essoufflées, au bout d'une course, arriver devant une fosse toute prête, et pas le temps de dire mot, pas le souffle.

Dites-moi, quel est donc le secret à ce propos?

7

Il y a constamment, lui dit-elle encore, des lions dans le village, qui se promènent sans gêne aucune. Moyennant qu'on ne fera pas attention à eux, ils ne font pas attention à nous.

Mais s'ils voient courir devant eux une jeune fille, ils ne veulent pas excuser son émoi. Non! Aussitôt ils la dévorent.

There are also agitations under the ground, and something like angers come to confront you in your house, like implacable beings who want to extort confessions.

Nothing can be seen, except what scarcely matters. Nothing, and yet we tremble. Why?"

6
"Each one of us here lives with her heart in her throat. Do you know that although I am very young, I used to be even younger, and the other girls were too. What does it mean? There's something about it that's dreadful.

And in those days when, as I said, we were even younger than now, we were afraid. They would have taken advantage of our confusion. They would have said, 'All right, we're burying you. Now is the time.' It's true we thought that could just as well happen this evening, if it's found to be the time.

And we didn't dare run too much: panting, at the end of a race, to stop on the edge of an open grave, and no time to utter a word, not enough breath.

Tell me, what is the secret about all this?"

7
"In the village," she says to him further, "there are always lions strolling about, entirely at ease. Providing we will pay no attention to them, they pay no attention to us.

But if they see a girl running, they are not inclined to excuse her for being alarmed. No! they devour her on the spot.

C'est pourquoi ils se promènent constamment dans le village où ils n'ont rien à faire, car ils bâilleraient aussi bien ailleurs, n'est-ce pas évident?

8

Depuis longtemps, longtemps, lui confie-t-elle, nous sommes en débat avec la mer.

De très rares fois, bleue, douce, on la croirait contente. Mais cela ne saurait durer. Son odeur du reste le dit, une odeur de pourri (si ce n'était son amertume).

Ici je devrais expliquer l'affaire des vagues. C'est follement compliqué, et la mer . . . Je vous prie, ayez confiance en moi. Est-ce que je voudrais vous tromper? Elle n'est pas qu'un mot. Elle n'est pas qu'une peur. Elle existe, je vous le jure; on la voit constamment.

Qui? Mais nous, nous la voyons. Elle vient de très loin pour nous chicaner et nous effrayer.

Quand vous viendrez, vous la verrez vous-même, vous serez tout étonné. "Tiens!" direz-vous, car elle stupéfie.

Nous la regarderons ensemble. Je suis sûre que je n'aurai plus peur. Dites-moi, cela n'arrivera-t-il jamais?

9

Je ne peux pas vous laisser sur un doute, continue-t-elle, sur un manque de confiance. Je voudrais vous reparler de la mer. Mais il reste l'embarras. Les ruisseaux avancent; mais elle, non. Ecoutez, ne vous fâchez pas, je vous le jure, je ne songe pas à vous tromper. Elle est comme ça. Pour fort qu'elle s'agite, elle s'arrête devant un peu de sable. C'est une grande

That's why there are always lions strolling around the village with nothing to do. Because obviously they could just as well yawn somewhere else, don't you think?"

8
"For a long, long time," she confides to him, "we've been in conflict with the sea.

Blue, sweet, once in a very great while you would think she was happy. But that never lasts. Besides, you can tell by the way she smells, rotten (unless it's her bitterness).

Now I should explain about the waves. It's incredibly complicated, and the sea . . . Do, please, trust me. Why would I want to mislead you? The sea isn't only a word. And she isn't only a fear. The sea—I swear to you—exists; one sees her all the time.

Who sees her? Why we do, we see her. She comes from a long way away to harass us and scare us.

When you're here, and can look for yourself, you'll be astonished. You'll say 'My!' you'll be so stunned.

We will look at the sea together. I'm sure I won't be afraid any more. Tell me, isn't that ever going to happen?"

9
"I don't want to leave you in doubt," she continues, "not knowing if you can believe me. Let me try again to tell you about the sea. But there's still the difficult part. Streams advance; she does not. Listen, don't be angry—I swear I wouldn't dream of misleading you. That's what the sea is like. Her most determined efforts give way to a little sand. She's

embarrassée. Elle voudrait sûrement avancer, mais le fait est là.

Plus tard peut-être, un jour elle avancera.

10
"Nous sommes plus que jamais entourées de fourmis," dit sa lettre. Inquiètes, ventre à terre elles poussent des poussières. Elles ne s'intéressent pas à nous.

Pas une ne lève la tête.

C'est la société la plus fermée qui soit, quoiqu'elles se répandent constamment au dehors. N'importe, leurs projets à réaliser, leurs préoccupations . . . elles sont entre elles . . . partout.

Et jusqu'à présent pas une n'a levé la tête sur nous. Elle se ferait plutôt écraser.

11
Elle lui écrit encore:

"Vous n'imaginez pas tout ce qu'il y a dans le ciel, il faut l'avoir vu pour le croire. Ainsi, tenez, les . . . mais je ne vais pas vous dire leur nom tout de suite."

Malgré des airs de peser très lourd et d'occuper presque tout le ciel, ils ne pèsent pas, tout grands qu'ils sont, autant qu'un enfant nouveau-né.

Nous les appelons des nuages.

always stumbling all over herself. She would certainly like to advance, but that's the fact.

Later on, perhaps, some day, she will advance."

10
"We're surrounded by ants more than ever," her letter says. "Nervous, going flat out, they push the dust around. They don't concern themselves with us.

Not one so much as lifts its head.

They're the world's most exclusive society, even though you can meet them far and wide. Just the same—the projects they want to get finished, their preoccupation . . . they keep to themselves . . . everywhere.

And to this day not one has lifted its head in our direction. They'd rather be stepped on."

11
She writes to him further:

"You can't imagine all there is in the sky. You have to see it to believe it. I mean, for example, the . . . but I'm not going to tell you their name just yet.

In spite of the way they look so imposing and take up nearly all of the sky, big as they are, they don't weigh even as much as a newborn baby.

We call them clouds.

Il est vrai qu'il en sort de l'eau, mais pas en les comprimant, ni en les triturant. Ce serait inutile, tant ils en ont peu.

Mais, à condition d'occuper des longueurs et des longueurs, des largeurs et des largeurs, des profondeurs aussi et des profondeurs et de faire les enflés, ils arrivent à la longue à laisser tomber quelques gouttelettes d'eau, oui, d'eau. Et on est bel et bien mouillé. On s'enfuit, furieuses d'avoir été attrapées; car personne ne sait le moment où ils vont lâcher leurs gouttes; parfois il restent des jours sans les lâcher. Et on resterait en vain chez soi à attendre.

12

L'éducation des frissons n'est pas bien faite dans ce pays. Nous ignorons les vraies règles et quand l'événement apparaît, nous sommes prises au dépourvu.

C'est le Temps, bien sûr. (Est-il pareil chez vous?) Il faudrait arriver plus tôt que lui; vous voyez, ce que je veux dire, rien qu'un tout petit peu avant. Vous connaissez l'histoire de la puce dans le tiroir? Oui, bien sûr. Et comme c'est vrai, n'est-ce pas! Je ne sais plus que dire. Quand allons-nous nous voir enfin?

Plume précédé de Lointain intérieur

It's true that they give out water, but not if you were to squeeze them or grind them up. It wouldn't be worth it, they hold so little.

But by means of extending themselves longer and longer, and wider and wider, and also deeper and deeper, and being as puffed up as they can be, they do in the long run manage to let fall a few little drops of water, yes, water. And one really and truly gets wet. Then we run, furious that we were caught; because nobody knows the moment when they are going to release their drops—sometimes they don't drop them for days. And it's no use staying at home to wait."

12
"Shivering is badly taught in this country. We don't know the real rules, and when it occurs we're always at a loss.

The problem is Time, of course. (Is it, where you live, too?) We'd have to get there ahead of it, if you see what I mean, just the least little bit ahead of it. Do you know the story about the flea in the drawer? Yes, of course you do. And how true that is, isn't it! I can't think what more to say. When are we going to see each other at last?"

P.T.

Bibliography

I. Nineteenth- and Twentieth-Century Poetry in France

A. Traditional Views

Balakian, Anna. *Literary Origins of Surrealism.* New York, King's Crown Press, 1947.

Boase, Alan M. *The Poetry of France, from Chénier to Pierre Emmanuel.* London, Methuen, 1952.

Chiari, Joseph. *Contemporary French Poetry.* Manchester, Manchester University Press, 1952.

Clancier, Georges-Emmanuel. *Panorama critique de Rimbaud au surréalisme.* Paris, Seghers, 1964.

Decker, Henry W. *Pure Poetry: 1925–1930.* Berkeley, University of California Press, 1962.

Gilman, Margaret. *The Idea of Poetry in France.* Cambridge, Harvard University Press, 1958.

Gutmann, René A. *Introduction à la lecture des poètes français.* Paris, Flammarion, 1961.

Quennell, Peter. *Baudelaire and the Symbolists.* 2nd rev. ed. London, Weidenfeld and Nicolson, 1954.

Raymond, Marcel. *De Baudelaire au surréalisme.* Edition nouvelle. Paris, J. Corti, 1966.

Richard, Jean-Pierre. *Poésie et Profondeur.* Paris, Editions du Seuil, 1955.

———. *Onze Etudes sur la poésie moderne.* Paris, Editions du Seuil, 1964.

B. Recent Views

Cohen, Jean. *Structure du langage poétique.* Paris, Flammarion, 1966.

Delas, Daniel, and Jacques Filliolet. *Linguistique et poétique.* Paris, Larousse, 1973.

Ducrot, Oswald, and Tzvetan Todorov. *Dictionnaire encyclopédique des sciences du langage.* Paris, Editions du Seuil, 1972.

Dufrenne, Mikel. *Le Poétique.* Paris, P.U.F., 1963.

Eco, Umberto. *L'Œuvre ouverte.* Paris, Editions du Seuil, 1965.

Garelli, Jacques. *La Gravitation poétique.* Paris, Mercure de France, 1966.

Greimas, A. J. et al. *Essais de sémiotique poétique.* Paris, Larousse, 1972.

Le Guern, Michel. *Sémantique de la métaphore et de la métonymie.* Paris, Larousse, 1973.

Levin, S. R. *Linguistic Structures in Poetry.* 's-Gravenhage, Mouton, 1962.

Meschonnic, Henri. *Pour la poétique.* Paris, Gallimard, 1970.

Riffaterre, Michael. *Essais de stylistique structurale.* Paris, Flammarion, 1971.

II. Works on French Versification

Grammont, Maurice. *Petit traité de versification française.* 20th ed. Paris, Armand Colin, 1964.

————. *Le Vers français.* 5th ed. Paris, Delagrave, 1964.

Guiraud, Pierre. *La Versification.* Paris, P.U.F., 1970.

Hytier, Jean. *Les Techniques modernes du vers français.* Paris, P.U.F., 1923.

Le Hir, Yves. *Esthétique et structure du vers français, d'après les théoriciens du XVIe siècle à nos jours.* Paris, P.U.F., 1956.

Lote, Georges. *Histoire du vers français.* Paris, Bavin, 1949.

III. Works on Rhetoric

Barthes, Roland. "L'ancienne rhétorique," *Communications,* 16, 1970.

Fontanier, Pierre. *Les Figures du discours.* Paris, Flammarion, 1968.

Groupe μ (J. Dubois, F. Edeline, J. M. Klinkenberg, P. Minguet, F. Pire, and H. Trinon). *Rhétorique générale.* Paris, Larousse, 1970.

Kuentz, P. "La rhétorique ou la mise à l'écart," *Communications,* 16, 1970.

Le Hir, Yves. *Rhétorique et stylistique de la Pléiade au Parnasse.* Paris, P.U.F., 1960.

Morier, Henri. *Dictionnaire de poétique et de rhétorique.* Paris, P.U.F., 1961.

Richards, I. A. *The Philosophy of Rhetoric.* New York, Oxford University Press, 1936.

IV. Works on Translation

Adams, Robert M. *Proteus, His Lies, His Truth.* New York, Norton, 1973.

Arrowsmith, William. *The Craft and Context of Translation.* Austin, University of Texas Press, 1961.

Boillot, Félix. *Le Vrai Ami du traducteur anglais-français et français-anglais.* Paris, P.U.F., 1930.

Brower, Reuben A. *On Translation.* Cambridge, Harvard University Press, 1959.

Langages, No. 23, 1972. On Translation.

Mounin, Georges. *Les Problèmes théoriques de la traduction.* Paris, Gallimard, 1963.

Selver, Paul. *The Art of Translating Poetry.* London, Baker, 1966.

V. Individual Poets: Works, Critical Editions, and Studies

Guillaume Apollinaire

Œuvres complètes. Paris, A. Balland and J. Lecat, 1965–66.

Breunig, LeRoy C. *Guillaume Apollinaire.* New York, Columbia University Press, 1969.

Carmody, Francis James. *The Evolution of Apollinaire's Poetics, 1901–1914.* Berkeley, University of California Press, 1963.

Davies, Marguerite. *Apollinaire.* Edinburgh, Oliver and Boyd, 1964.

Durry, Marie-Jeanne. *Guillaume Apollinaire, Alcools.* Paris, S.E.D.E.S., 1956–65.

Charles Baudelaire

Œuvres complètes. Ed. Y. G. Vanec and Claude Pichois. Paris, Bibliothèque de la Pléiade, 1935.

Les Fleurs du mal. Ed. Ernest Raynaud. Paris, Garnier, 1958.

Emmanuel, Pierre. *Baudelaire.* Paris, Desclée, De Brouwer, 1967.

Galand, René. *Baudelaire: poétique et poésie.* Paris, A. G. Nizet, 1969.

Peyre, Henri. *Baudelaire: a Collection of Critical Essays.* Englewood Cliffs, N.J., Prentice-Hall, 1962.

Pommier, Jean. *La Mystique de Baudelaire.* Geneva, Slatkine Reprints, 1967.

Sartre, Jean-Paul. *Baudelaire.* Paris, Gallimard, 1947. Translation of the above by Martin Turnell, Norfolk, Conn., New Directions, 1950.

Starkie, Enid. *Baudelaire.* Norfolk, Conn., New Directions, 1957.

Paul Eluard
Œuvres complètes. Paris, Gallimard, 1968.

Decaunes, Luc. *Paul Eluard.* Rodez, Editions Subervie, 1964.
Kittang, Atle. *D'Amour de poésie: essai sur l'univers des métamorphoses dans l'œuvre surréaliste de Paul Eluard.* Paris, Lettres modernes, Minard, 1969.
Perche, Louis. *Paul Eluard.* Paris, P.U.F., 1963.
Poulin, Gabrielle. *Les Miroirs d'un poète: image et reflets de Paul Eluard.* Bruxelles, Desclée, De Brower, 1969.

Jean Follain
Exister. Paris, Gallimard, 1947.
Chef-lieu. Paris, Gallimard, 1950.
Territoires. Paris, Gallimard, 1953.
Objets. Paris, Gallimard, 1955.
Tout instant, Poèmes en prose. Paris, Gallimard, 1957.
Des Heures. Paris, Gallimard, 1960.
D'après tout. Paris, Gallimard, 1967.

Dhotel, André. *Jean Follain.* Paris, Seghers, 1956.
Gavronsky, Serge. "Jean Follain" in *Poems and Texts.* New York, October House, 1969.

Jules Laforgue
Œuvres complètes. Ed. G. Jean-Aubry. Paris, Société du Mercure de France, 1922–62.

Durry, Marie-Jeanne. *Jules Laforgue.* Paris, Seghers, 1952.
Ramsey, Warren. *Jules Laforgue and the Ironic Inheritance.* New York, Oxford University Press, 1953.
————ed. *Jules Laforgue: Essays on a Poet's Life and Work.* Carbondale, Southern Illinois Press, 1969.
Ruchon, François. *Jules Laforgue, sa vie, son œuvre.* Geneva, A. Ciana, 1924.

Lautréamont
Œuvres complètes, Contenant les *Chants de Maldoror,* les *Poésies,* les *Lettres;* une introduction par A. Breton; des illustrations par Victor Brauner, Oscar Dominguez, Max Ernst, et al. Paris, G.L.M., 1938.

Bachelard, Gaston. *Lautréamont*. Paris, J. Corti, 1939.

Blanchot, Maurice. *Lautréamont et Sade*. Paris, Editions de Minuit, 1949.

Pleynet, Marcelin. *Lautréamont par lui-même*. Paris, Editions du Seuil, 1967.

Stéphane Mallarmé

Œuvres complètes. Texte établi et annoté par Henri Mondor et G. Jean-Aubry. Paris, Gallimard, 1970.

Cohn, Robert Greer. *Mallarmé's Un coup de dés: an exegesis*. New Haven, Yale French Publication, 1949.

——. *Towards the Poems of Mallarmé*. Berkeley, University of California Press, 1965.

Davies, Gardner. *Mallarmé et le drame solaire*. Paris, J. Corti, 1959.

Noulet, Edmond. *L'œuvre poétique de Stéphane Mallarmé*. Paris, E. Droz, 1940.

Richard, Jean-Pierre. *L'Univers imaginaire de Mallarmé*. Paris, Editions du Seuil, 1961.

Schérer, Jacques. *Le "Livre" de Mallarmé*. Paris, Gallimard, 1957.

Henri Michaux

Qui je fus. Paris, Editions de la N. R. F., 1927.

Mes Propriétés. Paris, Fourcade, 1929.

La Nuit remue. Paris, N. R. F., Gallimard, 1935.

Plume, précédé de *Lointain intérieur*. Paris, N. R. F., 1938.

Peintures, Paris, G. L. M., 1939.

L'Espace du dedans (1927–41). Paris, N. R. F., Gallimard, 1944.

Face aux verrous. Paris, N. R. F., Gallimard, 1954.

Vers la complétude. Paris, G. L. M., 1967.

Bellour, Raymoud, ed. *Les Cahiers de l'Herne*. No. 8. Paris, 1966.

Bertelé, René. *Henri Michaux*. Paris, Seghers, 1965.

Bréchon, Robert, *Michaux*. Paris, N. R. F., Gallimard, 1969.

Murat, N. *Michaux*. Paris, Editions universitaires, 1967.

Francis Ponge

Le Grand Recueil. Paris, Gallimard, 1961.

Tome Premier. Paris, Gallimard, 1965.

Pour un Malherbe. Paris, Gallimard, 1965.

Le Savon. Paris, Gallimard, 1967.

Nouveau Recueil. Paris, Gallimard, 1967.
La Fabrique du Pré. Geneva, Editions Skira, 1971.

Gavronsky, Serge. "Francis Ponge" in *Poems and Texts*. New York, October House, 1969.
Sartre, Jean-Paul. "L'Homme et les choses" in *Situations I*. Paris, Gallimard, 1947.
Sollers, Philippe. *Ponge*. Paris, "Poètes d'aujourd'hui," Seghers, 1963.
Spada, Marcel. *Francis Ponge*. Paris, "Poètes d'aujourd'hui," Seghers, 1974.
Thibaudeau, Jean. *Ponge*. Paris, Bibliothèque idéale, Gallimard, 1967.

Pierre Reverdy
La Plupart du temps (1915–22). Paris, Flammarion, 1967.
Main-d'œuvre (1913–49). Paris, Mercure de France, 1964.

Balakian, Anna. "Pierre Reverdy and the Materio-mysticism of Our Age" in *Surrealism*. New York, The Noonday Press, 1959.
Greene, Robert. *The Poetic Theory of Pierre Reverdy*. Berkeley, University of California Press, 1967.
Guiney, Mortimer. *La Poésie de Pierre Reverdy*. Geneva, Georg, 1966.
Rousselot, Jean. *Pierre Reverdy*. Paris, Seghers, 1951.

Arthur Rimbaud
Œuvres complètes. Ed. Rolland de Renéville. Paris, Bibliothèque de la Pléiade, 1951.
Œuvres. Ed. S. Bernard. Paris, Classiques Garnier, 1960.

Bonnefoy, Yves. *Rimbaud par lui-même*. Paris, Editions du Seuil, 1967.
Etiemble, René, et Yassu Gauclère. *Rimbaud*. Paris, N.R.F., Gallimard, 1950.
Py, Albert. *Illuminations*. Geneva, Librairie Droz, 1967.
Richard, Jean-Pierre. "Rimbaud ou la Poésie du devenir" in *Poésie et Profondeur*. Paris, Editions du Seuil, 1955.
Starkie, Enid. *Arthur Rimbaud*. New York, W. W. Norton and Co., 1947.

Jules Supervielle
Gravitations. Paris, Gallimard, 1925.
1939–1945. Paris, Gallimard, 1945.

La Fable du monde. Paris, Gallimard, 1950.
L'Escalier. Paris, Gallimard, 1956.
Le Corps tragique. Paris, Gallimard, 1959.
Le Forçat innocent suivi de *Les Amis inconnus.* Gallimard, Paris, 1969.

Etiemble, René. *Supervielle.* Paris, Gallimard, 1960.
Greene, Tatiana. *Jules Supervielle.* Geneva, E. Droz, 1958.
Hiddleston, James. *L'Univers de Jules Supervielle.* Paris, Corti, 1965.
Roy, Claude. *Jules Supervielle.* Paris, Seghers, 1949.

Paul Verlaine

Œuvres poétiques complètes. Ed. Y. G. Le Dantec. Paris, Bibliothèque
de la Pléiade, 1959.

Adam, Antoine. *Verlaine.* Paris, Hatier, 1966. Translation of the above
by Carl Morse. New York, New York University Press, 1963.
Nadal, Octave. *Paul Verlaine.* Paris, Société du Mercure de France.
1961.
Nicolson, Harold. *Paul Verlaine.* London, Constable and Company,
1921.
Richard, Jean-Pierre. "Fadeur de Verlaine" in *Poésie et Profondeur.*
Paris, Editions du Seuil, 1955.